Champs Elys

Palais de l'Elysée

Pl. des États Unis

Folies Marigny

Daudet

Amba d'Angl

R. Pierre

Égl. Amér

R. Égl. Grecque

Pal. de Glace

Av. Montaigne

Grand Palais des Beaux Arts

Petit Palais des Beaux Arts

Musée de Galliéra

R. Jean Goujon

Notre Dame de Consolation

Place d'Iéna

Trocadéro

Place de l'Alma

Cours la Reine

Pont Alex

Quai de la Conférence

Debilly

Pont de So

Quai

d Orsay

S E I N E

Port des Invalides

Écuries

Magasin des Hôpitaux Mil.

Manufact. des Tabacs

Gare des Invalides

Min. des Affaires Étrangès

de l'Université

Marché

Esplanade

R. St Dom

St Pierre

Pl. de Boui

Tour Eiffel

Rue de la Bourdonnais

R. St Dominique

Hospice Leprince

des

Invalides

Service géographique de l'armée

Grenelle

Pl. des Invalides

Palais Archiépiscop.

Min. et de l'In

Champ de Mars

Rue de Grenelle

Hôtel des Invalides

Min. Av.

Égl. St Louis des Invalid.

Boul. Latour Maubourg

Av. de la Motte-Picquet

Tombeau de Napoléon Ier

Rue de

Av. de Fourville

Place Vauban

Av. de la Fédération

Quartier de Cavalerie

Pl. Dupleix

R. Dupleix

École Militaire

Av. Lowendal

Sacré Cœur

R. Barbet de

Dupleix

Cloître des Armées

Pl. Fontenoy

St François-Xavier

Av. de

Caserne

R. Oudin

Inst. des Frères

Place Cambronne

Pl. Breteuil

Pasteur

Inst. des

Couvent des Visit

PARIS
COCKTAILS

THE ART OF FRENCH DRINKING

DONI BELAU

CIDER MILL
PRESS

BOOK
PUBLISHERS

KENNEBUNKPORT, MAINE

Paris Cocktails

13-Digit ISBN: 978-1604335637

10-Digit ISBN: 1604335637

This book may be ordered by mail from the publisher. Please include $4.95 for postage and handling. Please support your local bookseller first!

Books published by Cider Mill Press Book Publishers are available at special discounts for bulk purchases in the United States by corporations, institutions, and other organizations. For more information, please contact the publisher.

Cider Mill Press Book Publishers

"Where good books are ready for press"

12 Spring Street | PO Box 454

Kennebunkport, Maine 04046

Visit us on the Web! www.cidermillpress.com

Design by Jaime Christopher

"Joy Division" and "Sade's Taboo" from *Death & Co: Modern Classic Cocktails, with More than 500 Recipes* by David Kaplan, Nick Fauchald, and Alex Day, text copyright © 2014 by David Kaplan. Used by permission of Ten Speed Press, an imprint of the Crown Publishing Group, a division of Penguin Random House LLC. All rights reserved. Any third party use of this material, outside of this publication, is prohibited. Interested parties must apply directly to Penguin Random House LLC for permission.

Photos by Doni Belau: pages 25, 42, 46, 47, 52, 53, 55, 56, 72, 86, 88, 106, 112, 119, 121, 124, 131, 134, 138, 146, 154, 155, 178, 182 (top left), 189, 203, 204, 208, 210, 215, 216 (left), 220, 225, 248, 250, 264, and 267.

Courtesy of Melanie Vaz: page 99.

Courtesy of Bespoke: page 181.

Courtesy of Carina Tsou: pages 182 (bottom two rows), 185, 194, 195, 201, and 202.

Courtesy of Copper Bay: page 186.

Courtesy of Shake N' Smash: page 216 (right).

Courtesy of Death by Burrito: page 223.

Courtesy of Death & Co.: page 244.

Shutterstock images used under license: pages 1, 2, 3, 7, 14, 16, 21, 22, 26, 29, 33, 36, 39, 58, 61, 63, 65, 66, 70, 80, 85, 93, 96, 101, 102, 105, 111, 132, 140, 147, 149, 156, 159, 163, 167, 170, 177, 182 (top right), 206, 230, 237, 241, 242, 254, 255, 257, and 260.

iStock images used under license: pages 90 and 235.

Printed in China

2 3 4 5 6 7 8 9 0

- Contents -

Introduction • 4

J'Adore Paris Cocktails • 17

En Plein Air • 59

Du Vin • 73

Jazz Era Inspirations • 91

Casual and Creative
Cocktails • 141

Joyeuse Holidays • 157

Artisanal Cocktails • 171

Francophile in the USA • 231

Raising the Bar:
Best of the Best • 261

Acknowledgments • 265

Index • 267

About the Author • 271

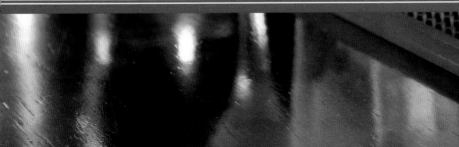

—INTRODUCTION—

THERE WAS THEN AND THERE IS NOW.

I've been coming to Paris since 1987 on an annual basis for weeks and now for months at a time. Back in those days, trying to get a barman to pour you a vodka on the rocks was so difficult; I once had to go back to the bar to point out the vodka bottle to the confused gent after three tries and three pours of gin on ice.

Then lightning hit, the cocktail heavens opened up and Romée de Gorianinoff and partners opened the Experimental Cocktail Club's speakeasy-style bar in 2007. La Conserverie and other craft bars opened in the following years, and now, craft cocktail culture is in full swing in Paris. You'll find that products are very carefully sourced; bitters, cordials and syrups are often handmade, and rums, whiskeys, and gins are macerated with exotic spices. This is the new "golden era" of Parisian cocktails—Parisians and visitors alike are waking up to a full-fledged cocktail craze.

Yet, is this entirely new? As the saying goes, what is old is new again. When Prohibition began in the States in 1919, some of the country's great bartenders hopped ship to Europe and became the Jazz Era's new mixologists. Frank Meier of the Ritz and Harry Craddock of the Savoy London come to mind. This was when the Bloody Mary, the French 75, and the Sidecar were invented, and you'll find a time much like now, when creativity was revered.

Think Hemingway packing a pistol and a strong drink or Cole Porter downing a bourbon after a night of playing.

Little known even by Parisian bartenders and bar owners is the fact that France actually has had a cocktail culture dating back to the 1800s. After talking to Stephen Martin at À La Française, who has been studying this issue for years now, I learned that in actuality France has had many hundreds of years relating in their own distinct way to their distilled liquors and liqueurs.

For the French palate three things are of utmost importance: alcohol is meant to go with food, balance in a drink is critical, and strong alcohol content in a drink feels alien and improper to them, because strong alcohol in France was typically used for medicinal purposes.

Take Chartreuse for example. Monks in the 1700s created Chartreuse Vert as a long life elixir. Bitters and eau de vies were taken for one's health or digestion often after a meal. In fact, there is a significant, age-old cultural difference in how the French perceive and understand liquor as opposed to how the Americans or the Brits comprehend it.

In France, liquor is not drunk to get drunk. So in essence, the idea of cocktailing is somewhat alien to them. The fact that the French don't like strong, alcohol-forward drinks doesn't make them newbie drinkers, rather it just shows that they come at the subject from a different perspective than an Anglo-Saxon. And I say, *vive la différence.*

At the turn of the century, cocktail bars were influenced greatly by expats and headquartered in the great hotels. Now the twenty- and thirty-somethings of France have embraced history only to remake it, in a more refined, more thoughtful way—and most importantly they are making this new cocktail culture much more accessible to the masses. We no longer just *prendre un verre* (have a glass), which in the past almost always meant wine. A French native today is open and anxious to try a French-made cocktail, chock full of French-made products.

With the exception of the five-star palace hotels, most of the well-made cocktails you'll sip in Paris are selling for 10 to 15 euros. That's expensive, it's true but it's still in the realm of reason when you consider the cost of the artisanal products that make up these creative cocktails and the time and care with which they are presented. We also hunted down a good batch of bars offering decent to excellent cocktails under 10 euros. And, to be sure, incredible things are still happening at the palace hotels. The Ritz and some of the newer five-star hotels have held their own due to wildly talented, professionally trained, passionate bartenders.

Today what we drink is art in a glass, and sipping these beauties turns a fun night of drinking into something exceptional and memorable. Fear not, for in our guide of Paris bars (new and historic) and Francophile bars in cities throughout the globe we have also included over 100 recipes so you can sample the artistry in your own home and bring a little corner of Paris into your life. For, where would we be without Paris?

> Look for the **C** and **V** icons next to recipe names throughout the book—the **C** identifies it is a craft cocktail recipe, and the **V** signals that it's a "vintage" recipe!

A Note About Ingredients (and Substitutions!)

The recipes in this book were taken verbatim from their creators. When a certain gin or rum is indicated, that brand was chosen by the mixologist because of the principles and the flavor profile of that liquor. The new craft bartenders take their ingredients very seriously, so if you want to replicate a drink exactly to be sure it tastes the same in your home as it does at the bar in Paris, use all the specific ingredients and brands listed. However, like a good mixologist will do when he or she runs out of something, feel free to substitute when necessary such as Absolut for Grey Goose vodka. Substituting your base liquor (e.g., gin, vodka, rum) with another premium brand is not going to hurt the outcome too much. However, having tasted the variety of different vermouths, liqueurs, and bitters (which is typically your secondary alcohol or flavor implement), there is a huge difference between them, and using a different brand in this case will make the drink taste quite different. Simply use your best judgment when substituting, and be sure to stock up on some key ingredients before tackling some of the more intricate recipes, like bitters and cordials! Happy mixing!

> "IF YOUR ARTERIES ARE GOOD, EAT MORE ICE CREAM. IF THEY ARE BAD, DRINK MORE RED WINE. PROCEED THUSLY."
>
> *Sandra Byrd, Bon Appétit*

> SIMPLE SYRUP: A number of cocktails call for simple syrup. Fortunately, simple syrup is as simple to make as its name suggests. Combine water and sugar in a 1:1 ratio and boil. As it boils, you'll see it become increasingly cloudy. Don't worry—by the time you're done, the syrup will be completely clear. That's how you know it's done. The syrup should keep for about a month in the fridge.

FRENCH COCKTAILING RULES

French love rules more than most cultures and as in everything else in French life, there are strict drinking guidelines to be followed.

DO clink glasses with everyone in the group, wishing each other "Santé"(to health).

DO NOT cross arms with others in your group—this brings bad luck.

DO make eye contact with the person whose glass you're clinking, or risk seven years of bad sex. Horrors!

DO bring a good bottle of champagne to your hostess.

DO NOT open the champagne before your guest of honor enters.

ALWAYS remember: moderation is a girl's best friend.

And the worst one, for me… Wait until a man at the table, preferably the host, pours you more wine.

P.S. I've always said rules were made to be broken.

– Cocktail Nomenclature –

Apéritif/Dijestif: A drink that stimulates your appetite or a drink that helps you digest your meal. Examples of apéritifs are Suze and soda, any champagne-based cocktail, Lillet or a kir. Dijestifs are drinks made with brandy, Chartreuse, Bénédictine, or calvados.

Bitters: There are two different categories of bitters. There bitter-flavored liqueurs, which are used as additions or as the base for a variety of cocktails. Examples include Campari, Suze, Aperol, Amaro, and Cocchi Rosa. There are also bitters, simply called *bitters*, which come in small bottles the most well known being Angostura bitters. These are infused and very flavorful alcohol-based liquids typically used in extremely small quantities to flavor a cocktail. They are made by a variety of companies and come in a myriad of flavors such as orange, chocolate, celery, and lavender, to name but a few.

> A NOTE ON BITTERS: Bitters are a key ingredient in today's craft cocktails. Stock up on a variety of flavors. There are a number of excellent companies making bitters in the U.S. and beyond including Bitter End, Fee's, Scrappy's, Bob's and Bittermans. Celery is one of the most common flavor profiles. A sampler pack, which several of the companies offer, is a great idea.

Cordials: A sweet substance made from fruit or flowers that is added to a cocktail or drank alone. In the United States, cordials are thought of as alcoholic and in the UK and elsewhere they are typically non-alcoholic.

Liqueur: An alcoholic substance that is typically sweeter than a liquor and made by combining a distilled spirit with something sweet and flavorful such as fruit, coffee, cream, chocolate, herbs, or spices. Examples are Cassis, Kahlúa, Irish cream, crème de menthe, and Grand Marnier.

VERMOUTH. Dry vermouth is white; sweet vermouth is red. France is more famous for its dry and Italy for its sweet. As in most things, the brand and quality matter.

LIQUOR: Alcoholic substance made from grains, plants, or sugar cane and fermented to be drunk straight or combined and used as the base of a cocktail. Examples are rum, vodka, gin, brandy, tequila, whiskey, and cachaça (a sugar cane–based alcohol made in Brazil).

SYRUPS: There is simple syrup, which is basically just sugar heated up in water so that it dissolves and then used to sweeten a drink, and flavored syrups, which are made in the same fashion but adding a flavor profile such as ginger, lemongrass, lime, or passion fruit. These are used to sweeten and add flavor to a cocktail. Some syrups can be bought over the counter; an example is Grenadine which is actually a pomegranate syrup.

WHAT IS THE CRAFT BAR MOVEMENT ALL ABOUT, REALLY?

Take the locavore movement, the artisanal quest, the DIY urge, and an ever-increasingly sophisticated palate. Combine that in a cocktail shaker with hundreds of specialized small-batch products made in France, garnish with passion and artistry, and you've got the Parisian craft bar movement.

It didn't start here, but with hundreds of years of experience distilling specialty liquors and liqueurs, France was ripe and waiting to fall head over heels into the movement. As Romée and his co-founders Olivier Bon and Pierre-Charles Cros from the Experimental Cocktail

Club group believed, if France has the best wine and food in the world, why not cocktails?

But Rome wasn't built in a day, and I don't want to give short shrift to those whose shoulders these new bartenders (both men and women) stand on. The guys from Le Grand Hotel bar, the Ritz, and of course Harry's New York bar were the beginners, then Le Forum opened in the '30s and Rosebud followed in the '60s.

Then in the 1990s, Buddha Bar hit the Parisian stage and almost singlehandedly was responsible for reintroducing exotic drinks and, more importantly, creating a global chic environment. Remember those lounge CDs that were an essential part of your CD collection, back when you actually had CDs?

The true beginning of the craft cocktail movement can be traced to 2000 when Milk and Honey opened in New York City and later to

2005 when Audrey Saunders opened the Pegu Club in Manhattan. All of these mixologists set the stage for 2007 when Experimental Cocktail Club opened in Paris just one year after Death & Company began in New York City in 2006. Paris and New York City drinkers were blown away by these adventurous bars that brought back the vintage look and feel of speakeasy days while putting a creative twist on the old recipes and revealing something entirely new.

Now bartenders are becoming as focused, diligent, and inventive as the most creative chefs in Paris, New York, London, Los Angeles, and beyond. They are using alcohol made from yogurt or tobacco, or infusing traditional alcohols with unusual spices or herbs. They are making their own shrubs, syrups, cordials, and bitters. Some of the most impressive drinks I tried were made with little-known fresh herbs, small-batch liqueurs and liquors; dehydrated orange or lemon slices or powdered dehydrated tomato laced around the rim of a Bloody Mary.

The garnishes have become terribly creative, pinned on with mini clothespins, referencing literature, or in a slight overstatement, set on fire. The worst of the bartenders were just mixing a lot of un-usual ingredients into something that tasted weird; the best were mixing a lot of unusual ingredients with some homemade products to create something sublime.

Everyone I met while researching this book had a passion for cocktail invention. While only a select few achieved a drink of Pi-casso or Matisse status, all are continuing to create with zeal. Gone are the days when a bar stool was simply a place to sit down and tell a guy your troubles while he poured you something strong. Now it's very tasty theatre, where bartender and patron alike are learning something new every day.

─ J'ADORE PARIS COCKTAILS ─

AMOUR À LA FRANÇAISE 20

SUZE AND SODA 24

LE METRO 27

ROSE COSMO 28

FRENCH 75 30

ROSE SALTY DOG 31

RITZ SIDECAR 33

ALCHIMIA COCKTAIL 37

VERBENA COCKTAIL 38

PARK HYATT PURPLE MOJITO 41

PERUVIAN SHRUB 43

TIJUANA SWIZZLE 44

B&B 45

OH MY DOG 48

100% WINTER VITAMIN 49

THE INCREDIBLE APICIUS
BLOODY MARY 54

RAPHAEL 57

G oing to over fifty bars in six weeks might not be everyone's idea of a good time, but I dare say a better education cannot be had if you really want to learn about the nature of bartending as it stands now in Paris. It's being called the "New Golden Age of Cocktails," and one cannot disagree considering how much passion, effort, sourcing and sheer love are being put into mixing these libations. These particular recipes are an homage to the most beautiful city on Earth. Cheers to drinking Paris in a glass!

"THE BEST OF AMERICA DRIFTS TO PARIS. THE AMERICAN IN PARIS IS THE BEST AMERICAN. IT IS MORE FUN FOR AN INTELLIGENT PERSON TO LIVE IN AN INTELLIGENT COUNTRY. FRANCE HAS THE ONLY TWO THINGS TOWARD WHICH WE DRIFT AS WE GROW OLDER—INTELLIGENCE AND GOOD MANNERS."

F. Scott Fitzgerald

C onceived at the Bar Le Forum, this brandy cocktail gets spiced up with ginger.

- 1⅓ oz. brandy
- ¾ oz. ginger liqueur
- 1 tablespoon lemon juice
- 1 tablespoon simple syrup
- 4 dashes of crème de Cassis
- White of one egg

METHOD: Shake all ingredients with ice in your cocktail shaker, and strain.

SERVING SUGGESTION: Serve in a Nick and Nora–style glass (a mini-martini glass with a rounded bottom) with a lemon twist.

"EVEN THE PIGEONS ARE
DANCING, KISSING,
GOING IN CIRCLES, MOUNTING
EACH OTHER.
PARIS IS THE CITY OF LOVE,
EVEN FOR THE BIRDS."

Samantha Schutz,
I Don't Want To Be Crazy

Midnight in Paris Party

It seems like everyone and her sister loved Woody Allen's "Midnight in Paris" from several years back. I believe that's because more than a few people fantasize about 1920s Paris, a magical time when Henry Miller, Dali, Josephine Baker, the Fitzeralds, and Hemingway roamed the streets. Ask all of your guests to dress up as one of the characters in the film, allowing just one choice per person so you don't have only Matisses running around.

Play the soundtrack to the film while you sip French 75s.

If the group demands it, sit down and watch the movie. If it's summer, borrow or rent a projector and play the DVD on a screen on your lawn and provide *beaucoup de* lawn chairs and blankets.

Serve:

Suze and Soda (page 24) • **Le Metro (page 27)** • **Rose Cosmo (page 28)** • **French 75 (page 30)**

Nibbles:

Mini baguette sandwiches. Cut the baguette into eighths, and serve with a variety of fillings such as pâté with cornichons, smoked salmon with cucumber and frisée, and *tradition mixte* (ham and cheese, such as Emmenthal with butter).

Present endive spears, celery, green onion, and carrot stalks served with a Roquefort dipping sauce (mix the cheese with crème fraiche and yogurt). Serve dip in a head of red radicchio with the middle cut out. For dessert, offer mini chocolate fondants.

Suze, a French brand of bitters, is surely as Parisian as a drink can be. Invented in the capital in the late 1800s, it tastes remarkably refreshing on the rocks with soda and an orange garnish.

• **1 portion of Suze**   • **3 parts soda water**

METHOD: Pour Suze and then soda into a rocks glass with ice.

SERVING SUGGESTION: Garnish with an orange wedge.

> A rocks glass, or a low-ball glass, is the type of glass in which a vodka, scotch, or a whiskey on the rocks is served, hence the name.

Bonheur, je te fais une grande place dans ma vie.

HAPPINESS. I MAKE A BIG SPACE FOR YOU IN MY LIFE.

M y friend Dana, who feels terribly lucky to be working as an American in France, created this one in honor of the fastest way to get around town. This is a version of the classic brandy cocktail, the Sidecar.

- 2 oz. high-quality French Brandy or Cognac (a very high-quality brandy is imperative)
- 1 oz. cassis
- ½ oz. lemon juice
- Several dashes of Pechaud bitters
- Morello cherries (or your favorite premium cherries)

METHOD: Shake all ingredients with ice in a cocktail shaker, strain, and serve in an ice-cold martini glass with two Morello cherries in Kirsch Liqueur.

"IF YOU ARE LUCKY ENOUGH TO HAVE
LIVED IN PARIS AS A YOUNG MAN,
THEN WHEREVER YOU GO FOR THE
REST OF YOUR LIFE, IT STAYS WITH
YOU, FOR PARIS IS A MOVEABLE
FEAST."

—Ernest Hemingway, A Moveable Feast

A floral take on the Sex in the City classic, courtesy of Jared Rapp from Dragon Bleu Vodka, made in France.

- **2 oz. Dragon Bleu Rose Vodka (or another brand of rose-flavored vodka)**
- **½ oz. triple sec or Cointreau**
- **½ oz. lime juice**
- **¾ oz. of cranberry juice**

METHOD: Pour all the ingredients in a cocktail shaker, and shake with ice until it's very cold.

Strain and place in a large frozen martini glass.

SERVING SUGGESTION: Garnish with a fresh organic rose petal.

JARED RAPP, CO-FOUNDER OF DRAGON BLEU VODKA MADE IN FRANCE

•••

"DRAGON BLEU IS MADE FROM WHEAT, BARLEY, AND RYE. THE FLAVOR PROFILE IS SLIGHTLY SWEET AND SPICY. IT'S REALLY A BIT DIFFERENT. I TEND TO THINK THAT IT'S SIMILAR TO BELVEDERE DUE TO THE RYE CONTENT, BUT IT REALLY STANDS ALONE. IT HAS WON THE TOP AWARD AND BEST IN SHOW IN ALMOST EVERY MAJOR COMPETITION."

This version of the classic invented at Harry's New York Bar in Paris in 1915 was re-created by Maxwell Britten at Maison Premiere.

- 1 oz. Dudognon 10 year
  (or your favorite cognac)
- ½ oz. fresh lemon juice
- ¼ oz. simple syrup
- Top with champagne

METHOD: Shake all ingredients save the champagne in your shaker with ice, strain, and serve in a champagne glass. Top with champagne.

VARIATION: Feel free to substitute any premium French cognac.

This is a French take on a classic cocktail. Crafted by Laura Morris in Paris.

- Himalayan pink salt
- 2 oz. Dragon Bleu Vodka (or your favorite premium vodka)
- 2¼ oz. fresh grapefruit juice
- ½ oz. Pamplemousse Rose Liqueur
- 1 barspoon Luxardo cherry

METHOD: Rim the glass with pink salt from the Himalayas.

Pour all ingredients into a high-ball glass with ice. Stir, and serve.

SERVING SUGGESTION: Garnish with a grapefruit peel twist.

"I DRINK TO MAKE OTHER PEOPLE MORE INTERESTING."

Ernest Hemingway

Although the Sidecar was invented in London, the Ritz made it famous (see Hemingway Bar at the Ritz, page 127). Courtesy of Colin Peter Field, Ritz Hotel.

- 2½ oz. cognac
- 1½ oz. triple sec or Cointreau
- 1 oz. lemon juice

METHOD: Stir all ingredients together in a glass with ice, strain, and serve on the rocks in a rocks glass with a lemon twist.

COLIN PETER FIELD, HEAD BARTENDER AT THE RITZ AND AUTHOR OF *BAR HEMINGWAY*

• • •

"IF A LADY IS WEARING BLACK, I'LL GIVE HER A RED OR WHITE ROSE AS A GARNISH FOR HER DRINK. IF SHE'S EXOTIC, I'LL PUT AN ORCHID IN HER COCKTAIL."

SHANGRI-LA

10 Avenue d'Iéna, 75116 Paris
Phone: 01 53 67 19 93
Price: ***
Atmosphere: Sophisticated
http://www.shangri-la.com/paris/

Drinks here will set you back some, but remember you'll be drinking in the former palace of Prince Roland Bonaparte, the grand-nephew of Napoleon (yes, *that* Napoleon). Don't go to the bar itself; instead, walk in boldly as if you were a guest and sit in one of the many intertwining rooms to your right. These were the palace's former parlor rooms and you'll find many comfortable places to sit. This is a beautiful

"I DRINK CHAMPAGNE WHEN I WIN, TO CELEBRATE.
AND I DRINK CHAMPAGNE WHEN I LOSE, TO CONSOLE MYSELF."

—*Napoleon Bonaparte*

area to have tea, but if you are ready for your cocktail, a waiter will come running. Order their 1896, a champagne cocktail that honors the year the palace was built. Dress appropriately, drink slowly, and enjoy thoroughly.

GEORGES V

33 Avenue George V, 75008 Paris
Phone: 01 53 23 78 52
Price: ***
Atmosphere: Regal
http://www.fourseasons.com/paris/
dining/lounges/le_bar/

I've always maintained that paying 25 euros or more for a cocktail here simply to sit among the incredible floral displays is worth it. Sometime back in 1999 Jeff Leatham, an American from Utah, was appointed head florist for the Four Seasons Georges V Hotel. The budget he was given was all but limitless. If you can imagine it, flowers appear here as theatre. They *will* take your breath away. And because it's the Four Seasons and one of the great hotels in Paris, the drinks will satisfy you, too. I prefer a champagne cocktail when I'm here because I want to feel like a princess in these surroundings.

Bar 228 at the Meurice

228 Rue de Rivoli, 75001 Paris
Phone: 01 44 58 10 66
Price: ***
Atmosphere: Perfect for planning how to conquer the world
www.lemeurice.com/

Here you'll pay a hefty sum for superb cocktails made by barman William Oliveri, who has been at the helm of Bar 228 for nearly three decades. Decorated like an English gentleman's club, you can hole up here sipping your vintage cocktail while pondering how you'll conquer the world. Or enjoy the Philippe Starck–designed lobby and have a drink at one of the comfy chairs.

Peninsula Hotel

19 Avenue Kléber, 75116 Paris
Phone: 1 58 12 28 88
Price: ***
Atmosphere: Grandiose
http://paris.peninsula.com

You have an embarrassment of choices at the Peninsula Hotel in terms of where to raise your glass. There's the rooftop terrace, the bar Kléber and the cigar lounge for after-dinner whiskey drinks, dijestifs and important discussions. With five-star service and cocktails, with your platinum card in hand you can't go wrong.

"TO ERR IS HUMAN.
TO LOAF IS PARISIAN."
Victor Hugo

Le Royal Monceau

228 Rue de Rivoli, 75001 Paris
Phone: 01 44 58 10 66
Price: ***
Atmosphere: Smart Upscale
http://www.leroyalmonceau.com/

Designed by Starck and owned by Raffles, this four-year-old palace hotel boasts an expansive bar made up of several rooms and a terrace, surprisingly subtle for Starck. But what's hiding in plain sight are some superbly delicious cocktails created by chef du bar Allessandro Cresto. I was wowed by my tasting at this bar, starting with the Singapore Sling (page 107), thankfully made less sweet than the norm.

Then I tasted the Verbena Cocktail (page 38), designed to celebrate spring and poured from a teapot. The herbal flavor mixing with the vodka and the citrus is a happy combination indeed.

Alchimia is the Italian word for *alchemy,* and there is no doubt that Alessandro from the Royal Monceau got it right here.

- 1¾ oz. Russian Standard Platinum Vodka
- ½ oz. cassis (preferably Mickael Antolin brand)
- ½ oz. galangal syrup (see instructions below)
- ¾ oz. fresh lemon juice
- 1¼ oz. infusion of lemon balm, verbena, cinnamon, and orange peel

METHOD: To make galangal syrup, add some slices of the Asian ginger plant galangal (see photo on opposite page) to your simple syrup while boiling. When creating the syrup, let stand for as long as possible to soak up the taste.

Make the infusion by putting the fresh herbs, spices, and orange peel in boiling water and let it steep like tea. The longer you steep the more fragrant the infusion, then let cool before using.

Vigorously shake all of the ingredients above in a cocktail shaker with ice to make a nice foam, then pour into a martini glass.

SERVING SUGGESTION: Garnish with one cucumber slice and fresh verbena leaves.

— VERBENA COCKTAIL —

Created by Alessandro behind the bar at the Le Royal Monceau, Paris.

- 1¾ oz. Beefeater 24 gin infused with verbena leaves
- 1 tablespoon lavender syrup
- 2 teaspoons Velvet Falernum
- 1 oz. apple juice

TO INFUSE THE GIN: Infuse 1 liter of gin with ¼ cup of lemon verbena leaves for at least 24 hours but up to 4 days. Strain before using.

TO MAKE LAVENDER SYRUP: Make simple syrup but add a dried handful of lavender flowers while boiling the sugar, let steep, strain, and use once cold.

Now you'll be ready to make several Verbena Cocktails. To make one, put all the ingredients in a small pitcher and mix them with ice.

SERVING SUGGESTION: Let the recipient pour over ice in a rocks glass with fresh verbena leaves and large ice cubes.

PARK HYATT VENDOME

19 Avenue Kléber, 75116 Paris
Phone: 1 58 71 10 60
Price: ***
Atmosphere: Slick chic
http://paris.vendome.hyatt.com

Somewhere between slick and cozy, catering to a crowd of hotel guests and Parisians, the bar at the Vendome Hotel will never remind you of a Hyatt back home. This is a five-star experience, and the cocktail prices, which run from 27 to 30 euros, will prove it. Sit at the bar to enjoy the extremely experienced barmen and women who will present you with truly unique drinks. I tried the Tijuana Swizzle with Mezcal (page 44), but if you want something lighter try the Bramble & Queen (page 113) served in one of the most gorgeous coupe glasses I've ever seen. This drink incorporates ylang ylang water and will transport you to an exotic beach in Asia.

YANN DANIEL,

HEAD BARTENDER

AT PARK HYATT VENDOME

• • •

"FOR FRENCH PEOPLE, TEQUILA HAS A BAD IMAGE. BEFORE, NO ONE EVER DRANK GOOD TEQUILA AND EVERYONE HAS A STORY OF A BAD NIGHT WITH THIS ALCOHOL. THIS IS WHY WHEN I CREATE A DRINK WITH TEQUILA OR MEZCAL, I MUST USE THE FINEST PRODUCTS, AND IT MUST TASTE SPECTACULAR."

Mojitos are the go-to drinks for all Parisians and newbie cocktail enthusiasts. Most of the craft bars turn up their noses at the ubiquitous cocktail, but here Yann Daniel from the Park Hyatt Vendome offers up a more interesting solution.

* 4 fresh blackberries
* 12 mint leaves
* Half of a fresh lime
* 2 barspoons of brown sugar
* Soda water
* 1 tablespoon violet syrup (or crème de violette)
* 1¾ oz. Bacardi reserve dark rum

METHOD: Muddle the blackberries, the mint leaves, lime, and sugar together with a little bit of soda water in a high-ball glass.

Pour in the violet syrup and the dark rum. Fill the glass with crushed ice and top off with soda water.

SERVING SUGGESTION: Stir it with a barspoon, and add mint leaf garnish and two straws (two straws make it easier to continue to muddling action on your own).

— PERUVIAN SHRUB —

This unique cocktail invented by Yann Daniel at the Park Hyatt Vendome bar should be served in a Japanese-style glass, something you might use for green tea but filling it with ice instead.

- 1¾ oz. Pisco
- 1 oz. Red fruits shrub
- ½ oz. fresh apple juice
- 2 teaspoons Cherry Heering liqueur
- 1 dash of Rhubarb bitters
- ½ oz. Corona beer

METHOD: Pour all the ingredients into the shaker, and refresh the cocktail using the Cuban roll technique. The Cuban roll technique is done by pouring your ingredients into a pint-size glass with ice and then pouring them into your cocktail shaker, moving back and forth. Not a shake or stir, this method incorporates the ingredients without melting too much ice.

Then strain into your Japanese-style glass filled with ice.

SERVING SUGGESTION: Garnish with red fruits such as raspberries or strawberries, mint leaves, and a straw.

A shrub is flavored simple syrup with vinegar added. A company named Shrub & Co. makes a strawberry shrub which would work well in this recipe. To make your own red fruits shrub, take ½ cup of white wine vinegar and ½ cup of sugar and heat adding ½ cup of strawberries or raspberries or a combination of the fruits. Simmer while the fruit releases its juices. Strain and store in a jar in the fridge for several days at which time it will be fully infused. This mixture should keep for quite some time.

— TIJUANA SWIZZLE —

The Tijuana Swizzle is much more interesting and complex than your typical tequila drink, designed for a more sophisticated palate by Yann Daniel at the Park Hyatt Vendome bar.

- 4 coffee beans
- 2 oz. Mezcal Vida
- 1 tablespoon homemade pepper syrup
- ¾ oz. apricot juice
- ¾ oz. lime juice
- 1 tablespoon Bénédictine
- 1 tablespoon ginger cordial
- 5 dashes Angostura bitters

METHOD: Muddle coffee beans in a high-ball glass, then add all the liquid ingredients except the Angostura bitters, fill the glass with crushed ice, and stir it well using a swizzle stick.

Add the Angostura bitters on the top to get a darker layer and refill the glass with crushed ice.

SERVING SUGGESTION: The Vendome garnishes this drink with lime peel, star anise, a cinnamon stick, a coffee bean, and a small red pepper, arranged in a beautiful way with two straws.

A classic vintage drink and an ideal dijestif, using Bénédictine liqueur, which was invented more than five centuries ago.

• **1 part Bénédictine liqueur**   • **1 part Brandy**

Serve on the rocks in a rock glass. Mix with a barspoon.

> Bénédictine liqueur made in France has been imported to the States since the late 1800s but was created in the early part of the 1500s by a Bénédictine monk as a medicinal tonic. Bénédictine was used in a popular vintage drink, the B&B, created in the 1930s.

> This classic cocktail was typically made with 3 Barrels Brandy, but I'd suggest using Hennessey, Delamain, or Martell Cognac.

Le Quatre

Buddha Bar Hotel, 4 Rue d'Anjou, 75008 Paris

Phone: 01 83 96 88 70

Price: ***

Atmosphere: Exclusive & intimate

http://www.buddhabarhotelparis. com/

The bar inside the Buddha Bar Hotel was designed to be very different than the über-famous original Buddha Bar, which is around the corner. The original that opened in 1996 with the gigantic Buddha is a huge place with setups behind the bar for up to five bartenders. Now there are fourteen Buddha bars worldwide. This iconic place is nearly single-handedly responsible for the Lounge CD trend that was omnipresent in the late 1990s and early 2000s. Mathias, who heads up the Buddha bars around the world, helped create this smaller, more intimate bar in the five-star hotel. You can enjoy tea here in the afternoon and some killer drinks at night, such as their popular Oh My Dog. In fine weather, take your drink in the beautiful courtyard and say a toast of gratitude.

MATHIAS GIROUD,
WORLDWIDE MANAGER
OF BUDDHA BAR

• • •

"OUR COCKTAILS ARE
MEANT TO TRANSPORT
YOU TO AN EXOTIC
PLACE."

— OH MY DOG —

This popular cocktail is served at both the Buddha Bar Paris and the Buddha Bar Hotel bar, Le Quatre.

- **1¾ oz. gin infused with white pepper**
- **½ oz. Grenade liquor**
- **½ tablespoon Belvoir raspberry and rose cordial**
- **Ginger ale to top**
- **Grenadine**
- **Wedge of fresh lime**

METHOD: To infuse gin with white pepper, place ½ tablespoon of white peppercorns (broken) in 1 liter bottle of gin for 5 hours. Strain before using.

Combine infused gin, grenadine, and cordial in a cocktail shaker with ice, shake, strain, and serve with ice in a lovely tumbler topping with ginger ale.

SERVING SUGGESTION: Garnish with a shake of grenadine and fresh lime.

> Belvoir produces a delightful raspberry and rose cordial made in the UK that you can get in the States. In this case, the word *cordial* is used to identify a sweet, non-alcoholic drink. If you cannot find it in your region, substitute a drop of rosewater and several crushed raspberries, being careful to strain out the seeds before serving over ice and topping off with the ginger ale.

This actually feels healthy when you drink it, thanks to the guys at the Buddha Bar Paris. Serve at brunch.

- 1¾ oz. vodka
- 2 teaspoons Cynar
- 2 teaspoons Aperol
- 2 teaspoons honey (or less if you don't like it very sweet)
- 2 teaspoons lime
- 2 barspoon apricot/yuzu jam
- 1¾ oz. juice made from fresh carrot and fresh apple (half and half—store-bought juice is fine)
- 2 dashes of celery bitters

METHOD: Shake all ingredients with ice, strain, and serve in a small carafe or soup style.

SERVING SUGGESTION: Top with finely chopped carrot shavings and green leaves such as coriander or parsley.

> Cynar, similar to Campari, is a bitter liqueur made in Italy from artichokes as well as other ingredients. Don't worry, it doesn't taste like artichokes!

CHEZ PRUNE

36 Rue Beaurepaire, 75010 Paris
Phone: 01 42 41 30 47
Price: *
Atmosphere: Bobo central

This was one of the first really cool places to open on the Canal St. Martin. Look no further if you are on the hunt for the quintessential Parisian bobo, otherwise known as a hipster; they hang out here in droves. This place is all about the bohemian "scene" and is an embarrassment of riches when it comes to people watching.

"I'VE GOT LOTS OF GOOD FRIENDS. I COULD HAVE AFFAIRS. I CAN READ A BOOK ALL NIGHT, PUT THE CAT ON THE END OF THE BED. I CAN PICK UP MY PASSPORT AND GO TO FRANCE. I DON'T HAVE TO ASK ANYBODY."

—*Joanna Lumley*

CIEL DE PARIS

33 Avenue du Maine, 75015 Paris
56th floor
Phone: 0 1 40 64 77 64
Price: ***
Atmosphere: Elite view
http://www.cieldeparis.com/

If you want champagne and a city view, this is the best place in town. You'll also find an impressive array of champagnes by the glass from 13 to 30 euros as well as Bellini's, including one champagne cocktail with mandarin and ginger.

LA BELLE HORTENSE

31 rue Vieille du Temple, 75004 Paris
Phone: 01 42 74 59 70
Price: **
Atmosphere: Literary chic
http://www.cafeine.com/
belle-hortense

This has been one of my favorite bars for forever. It's small and terribly French, with the fantasy bohemian French chic décor that we all love—plus it's a bookstore. To me, this is a naturally perfect combination. The owner, Xavier Denamur, has about six places around Paris including two more on the same street; each has its own flavor but every one is similarly charming. (See website for details.)

LAPÉROUSE

51 Quai des Grands Augustins, 75006 Paris
Phone: 1 43 26 68 04
Price: ***
Atmosphere: Late-night rendez-vous
http://www.laperouse.com/

This 250-plus-year-old bar and restaurant is famous not only for its extremely beautiful interior but also for its private rooms upstairs. This is where the gentlemen of the day used to bring their courtesans or mistresses and give them diamonds to keep them bejeweled. You'll see scratch marks still on the old mirrors in these elite little private rooms because the mademoiselles wanted to be sure the diamonds were indeed real.

LA RECYCLERIE

83 Boulevard Ornano, 75018 Paris
Phone: 01 42 57 58 49
Price: *
Atmosphere: Eco-friendly
http://www.larecyclerie.com/

Although not situated in the most pristine area of Paris, this restaurant/bar/farm is buzzing with life inside the old train station it calls home. During the summer, sip your cocktails on the long stretch of terrace that parallels the old railroad tracks and enjoy this eclectic and creative space in Montmartre.

L'APICIUS

20 Rue d'Artois, 75008 Paris
Phone: 1 43 80 19 66
Price: ***
Atmosphere: Refined
http://restaurant-apicius.com/

Situated in a corner of the 8th arrondissement in a beautiful mansion from the 1860s is a Michelin Star restaurant and a very chic bar with a tiny terrace that you can enjoy even if you aren't prepared to pay for a meal here. The 19th-century frescoed ceilings in

the bar somehow meld perfectly with the modern, dramatic décor, but the real star here, eclipsing the gorgeous surroundings, are the *sur mesure* cocktails prepared by the talented *chef du bar*, Valentin. Tell him or the bar manager Jil what you are in the mood for; don't be too specific but do try to challenge them. Or try their farm-to-glass Bloody Mary, made with cherry tomatoes smashed and strained in front of your eyes with BBQ bitters and cranberries. Yes, I said it: cranberries?! You'll never taste anything else like it. Refreshing, smoky, salty, and not nearly as thick as some Bloody's—this is a triumph!

L'ÉCLAIR

32 Rue Cler, 75007 Paris
Phone: 1 44 18 09 04
Price: **
Atmosphere: Cozy & bohemian
http://www.leclairparis.com/

If you want to party and have a proper drink in the 7th arrondissement, L'Eclair is your best choice. This bohemian chic stop on the rue Cler complete

with a cozy terrace, is open for breakfast, lunch, and dinner, but the surprise is the intellect behind the bar. Yes, they offer some sweeter stuff for cocktail newbies, but Sulyman the barman is making his own bitters, curing his own rum, and taking his job seriously. His spin on the cucumber martini is perfection, and for something a bit sweeter but still balanced, try the Porn Star Martini with passion fruit and a shot of champagne! Hopefully, it's the only time you and this phrase are mentioned in the same sentence.

Valentin, one of the most talented bartenders in Paris, created this for the Apicius bar and restaurant, which serves them by the handful at lunch. Try one and you'll see why. It's very different from a standard Bloody because it uses fresh tomatoes, and it is impossible to put down.

- 1 cup of cherry tomatoes
- 4 drops Tabasco Chipotle flavor
- 2 dashes white balsamic cream
- 1¾ oz. cranberry juice
- ¾ oz. vodka
- 2 turns of a pepper mill
- 3 drops Memphis BBQ bitters by Bitter End
- Celery salt

METHOD: In a Boston shaker, crush cherry tomatoes, add Tabasco Chipotle, balsamic cream, cranberry juice, vodka, 2 turns of the pepper mill, 3 pinches of celery salt, and the Memphis bitters. Shake strongly for 20 seconds, double strain, and serve in a chilled martini glass.

SERVING SUGGESTION: Decorate the rim with celery salt, 1 cherry tomato, and one grind of the pepper mill (white pepper is preferred).

White Balsamic Cream is available from gourmet food distributors online.

RAPHAEL TERRACE

17 Avenue Kléber, 75116 Paris
Phone: 01 53 64 32 00
Price: ***
Atmosphere: Inviting
http://www.raphael-hotel.com/

Hiding inside this somewhat staid hotel are two secrets. First, downstairs in the English gentleman's bar, which has been virtually untouched since the opening of the hotel in 1924, you'll find the spot where the late French singer and cultural icon Serge Gainsberg spent his nights drinking Gibsons. Upstairs, in fine weather, call ahead and book a table with a bottle of champagne or wrestle through the crowd to get a much-coveted seat on the roof with a view of all of Paris. Yes, it's worth the fight, and once settled, Christian Gomez, the chef du bar, will treat you like you belong.

This signature drink at the rooftop bar at the Raphael hotel is fresh and breezy.

- 2 oz. strawberry puree
- ½ oz. Manzana Verde
- 1 tablespoon fresh lime juice
- Brut Champagne to top

METHOD: Shake strawberry puree, Manzana Verde, and lime juice together together into a cocktail shaker with ice, and strain.

SERVING SUGGESTION: Serve in a chilled champagne glass, topping off with Brut champagne. Garnish with a strawberry.

Manzana Verde is a green apple liqueur made by a number of companies, including Briottet and Giffard, which are good French brands.

ICED TEA PEYI 62

MACARONI COCKTAIL 67

BISOUS DU SOLEIL 68

ROSE DE VARSOVIE 71

Drinking outdoors in Paris is magical. To *prendre un verre* and indulge in some people watching or view-goggling is a pastime that is taken seriously in all seasons by Parisians and visitors alike.

V

Imagine you are a sailboat sailing around Martinique when you sip this one, coming to us via Michael at Maria Loca (page 225).

- 1½ oz. White Agricole Rhum or Cachaça Prata (or your favorite rum)
- 1¾ oz. hibiscus water or agua de Jamaica
- 2 teaspoons Gomme syrup (or simple syrup)
- 1 tablespoon lime juice
- 1 tablespoon Velvet Falernum
- 1 dash Peychaud bitters

METHOD: Put all ingredients in a cocktail shaker with ice, shake, and serve on ice in a rocks glass.

SERVING SUGGESTION: Garnish with a round of lime.

Gomme syrup is slightly different than regular simple syrup and can be purchased, but feel free to substitute simple syrup here.

"FOR ART TO EXIST, FOR ANY SORT OF AESTHETIC ACTIVITY OR PERCEPTION TO EXIST, A CERTAIN PHYSIOLOGICAL PRECONDITION IS INDISPENSABLE: INTOXICATION."

Friedrich Nietzsche

Provençal Party

The setting must be the countryside. It is preferable to set out a long wooden table and cover it with a sweet country tablecloth, something clean but not too fancy. Don't make the mistake of using your patio furniture; it is simply not the same.

Bring out mismatched cups and glasses and napkins. An old pitcher of flowers you've picked will make a delightful centerpiece.

After some drinks and some nibbles, take naps on old blankets in the summer sunshine.

SERVE:

Pastis is *the* drink in the South of France; the licorice liqueur (see photo on the opposite page), is normally served on ice, then water is added. Here we're going to step it up a notch and serve it in Macaroni Cocktails (page 67). The taste of licorice is very refreshing on a sunny day. However some of your guests may prefer a **Bisous du Soleil** (page 68) or a **Rose de Varsovie** (page 71).

NIBBLES:

Lay out both **salmon pâté** and a **country pâté** and cut up some **baguette** (the French never serve crackers with pâté so you shouldn't either). Make sure to have a good bowl of olives available such as Lucques. **Crudités** with aioli dipping sauce will strike the right note. After a few cocktails, resort to rosé wine to turn it down a notch. If you wish to serve a proper lunch, several varieties of quiche with a big green salad will work well.

"I LIKE THE EIFFEL TOWER BECAUSE IT LOOKS LIKE STEEL AND LACE."

Natalie Lloyd

— MACARONI COCKTAIL —

This fun drink was originally served with absinthe.

- 1 oz. pastis of your choice (Ricard and Pastis 51 are the most common brands)

- ½ oz. sweet vermouth (Carpano and Cocchi are nice Italian brands—or Dolin, which is made in France)

METHOD: Shake pastis and sweet vermouth with ice and strain into a small very cold Moroccan tea glass.

— BISOUS DU SOLEIL —

ruity but not too sweet, perfect for sipping on a sunny day in the French countryside. Created by Krystal Kenney, Paris.

- 1 oz. vodka
- Dash of Cointreau (or your preferred triple sec)
- 1½ oz. cranberry juice
- Juice of ½ lime
- Juice from 1 orange wedge
- Add a twist of orange
- Fill with champagne

METHOD: Combine vodka, Cointreau, and the juices in a cocktail shaker with ice. Shake and strain.

SERVING SUGGESTION: Serve in a coupe glass with a twist of orange and top off with champagne.

> A coupe glass is an old-fashioned champagne glass in the shape of Marie Antoinette's breasts—an old wives' tale but a good one.

Hôtel Particulier Bar

23 Avenue Junot, Pavillon D, 75018 Paris
Phone: 01 53 41 81 40
Price: ***
Atmosphere: Secret garden
http://hotel-particulier-montmartre.com/

Hidden down a little path next to a petanque court in the rear of the Hôtel Particulier, is a secret little outdoor haven for drinks in the summer behind the hotel of the same name. A more romantic spot cannot be found. Read the directions carefully on the website, or you'll never find this little gem. If you want to have an illicit affair, this is the spot; there are even hotel rooms upstairs should the mood be right.

Le Mini Palais

3 Avenue Winston Churchill, 75008 Paris
Phone: 01 42 56 42 42
Price: ***
Atmosphere: Magical
http://www.minipalais.com/

For one of the best views in Paris, grab a seat on the terrace of Le Mini Palais, the restaurant and bar situated in the same building as the Grand Palais and directly across from the Petit Palais. This is not a rooftop view; the terrace is only a few floors up but enjoys a stunning view of the Petit Palais in its Art Nouveau and Neo Baroque splendor. While the restaurant itself is quite modern and a bit stark, the terrace is enchanting and is an ideal place to spend a warm evening enjoying a drink or two.

Le Perchoir

14 rue Crespin du Gast, 75011 Paris
Phone: 01 48 06 18 48
Price: **
Atmosphere: Aerial
http://leperchoir.fr

Le Perchoir was the *it* place of 2013 and 2014 and ushered in the rooftop bar scene in Paris. It's not as if there was never before a rooftop that served drinks, but they were mostly found in hotels. There are several bars, one on the roof and another on the sixth floor. The people-watching is divine, DJs are talented, and cocktails by Luther are cold and refreshing. This is the place to be on a hot night.

Le Forum's rose-colored cocktail, so ladylike and lovely.

- 1¾ oz. vodka
- ½ oz. Peter Heering Cherry liqueur
- 4 drops de Cointreau (or your preferred triple sec)
- 3–4 drops of Angostura bitters

METHOD: Place all ingredients in a glass and stir with ice for about 15 seconds.

Strain and serve in a chilled or frozen martini glass.

SERVING SUGGESTION: Garnish with a Morello kirsch cherry.

— DU VIN —

KIR ST. LOUIS 76

ROSÉ-PAMP 77

MADAME ROUGE 78

SHERRY CHERIE 79

THE BASTILLE CELEBRATION 82

SERENDIPITI 83

CORPSE REVIVER NO. 2 84

A traditional apéritif in France has *toujours* been *un verre de champagne*. True, it's hard to go wrong ordering that, but due to the country's love for wine and champagne, there is an inordinate amount of superb recipes presented in Paris bars using champagne and other wines to "top off" a cocktail, making the drink a sparkling adventure.

One would be remiss not mentioning an important part of the Parisian drinking scene: wine bars. They've been around forever, but wine bars serving uniquely (or a least some) natural wine has been the craze for almost a decade now.

Wine bars—and wine and champagne cocktails—are a great way to start, end, or sit one's night out (or in!) when you need a little break from your cocktails.

"CHAMPAGNE IS ONE OF THE ELEGANT EXTRAS IN LIFE."

—Charles Dickens

This twist on the Kir was created by friends at my apartment on the Ile St. Louis.

- ½ oz. St. Germain (or other elderflower liqueur)
- 1 oz. Pamplemousse Rose liqueur
- Champagne to fill

METHOD: Pour elderflower liqueur and Pamplemousse in a champagne glass, and top with champagne.

SERVING SUGGESTION: Serve in a champagne glass with a horse's neck grapefruit rind.

> A horse neck twist is created by cutting the citrus (lemon, grapefruit, or lime) with a sharp pairing knife around in a circle while spinning the fruit to create a long spiral.

A perfect summery cocktail for a shady spot on a summer day.

- 1 oz. Pink Grapefruit Liqueur
  (Edmond Briottet grapefruit
  liqueur is a good brand)
- 4 oz. cold rosé wine

METHOD: Combine the liqueur and wine and serve in a chilled wine glass.

> *Le plus lourd fardeau,*
> *c'est d'exister sans vivre.*
>
> **THE GREATEST BURDEN IS TO**
> **EXIST WITHOUT LIVING.**
> **—VICTOR HUGO**

There is something about that lady in red.

- **2 oz. Brenne Whisky (or another smooth non-peaty whisky)**
- **1 oz. Amaro**
- **2 oz. Brut Sparkling Wine**

METHOD: Stir whisky and Amaro together with ice, and strain into a chilled champagne flute.

SERVING SUGGESTION: Top with sparkling wine and serve.

"THREE BE THE THINGS I SHALL NEVER ATTAIN: ENVY, CONTENT, AND SUFFICIENT CHAMPAGNE."

—*Dorothy Parker*

Created by Jen Riley at the Red House, this unique champagne cocktail has French and Portuguese elements plus a hint of the tropics.

- 1½ oz. Amontillado Sherry
- 1 tablespoon dry curaçao, preferably Pierre Ferrand (or your favorite orange-flavored liqueur)
- 2 teaspoons simple syrup
- 1 oz. tamarind water
- Chilled dry champagne to top

METHOD: Build this cocktail straight into a highball style glass over ice, stir, and top off with champagne.

SERVING SUGGESTION: Garnish with a sprig of rosemary.

Tamarind is a sweet and sour fruit found in Southeast Asia. Buying tamarind paste is quite easy online or at an Indian or Asian market. Use 2 teaspoons of the paste with ¾ cup of hot water to dissolve. Cool down and strain before using. The closest substitute for tamarind water would be diluted lime juice, but it won't be quite the same.

Sparkling Fête

This is a French-themed artsy party that is perfect to celebrate an engagement, the birth of a baby, a big birthday party, or even New Year's!

Buy a gigantic piece of poster board, or better yet, stretch and temporarily pin some canvas across a blank wall. Provide a set of pastels and charcoal. After handing a guest one of the champagne cocktails you have on offer, ask them to draw some good wishes for the happy couple, the New Year, or whatever you are celebrating. This can be given to the person(s) of honor as a parting gift.

SERVE:

- **A whiskey-based champagne cocktail, the Bastille Celebration (page 82)**
- **The Serendipiti, made with Calvados (page 83)**
- **A Pernod-based vintage Champagne cocktail, the Corpse Reviver No. 2 (page 84)**

NIBBLES:

FRENCH HERB DIP served in a half of a red pepper with crudités. To make the herb dip: Combine a soft goat cheese with fresh herbs (like chervil, parsley, chives and tarragon), add herbes de Provence, yogurt, sour cream, and lemon zest until consistency and flavor is just right.

OYSTERS ON THE HALF-SHELL (from Normandy if you can get them). Serve with a *piment d'espelette* sauce:

- 1 tablespoon finely chopped shallot
- 2 teaspoons fresh lemon juice
- 2 teaspoons white wine wine vinegar
- 1 cup mayonnaise
- 1 teaspoon piment d'Espelette
- Coarse sea salt
- Freshly ground black pepper

- **Salmon rillettes (make or buy)**
- **Escargot with warm crusty bread**
- **A superb selection of French chocolates, or make your own cognac truffles**

Does your evening call for a celebration? This lovely concoction should do the trick.

- **2 oz. Bastille Whisky**
- **A splash of St. Germain (or other elderflower liqueur)**

- **Champagne**

METHOD: In a chilled champagne glass, combine the whisky and liqueur, and then fill with champagne.

SERVING SUGGESTION: Garnish with a raspberry or a strawberry.

> This is an easy drink for someone who doesn't know that they like whisky… yet.

Colin Peter Field, chef du bar at the Ritz, says this is his favorite drink.

- **1 oz. Calvados (or your apple brandy of choice)**
- **A sprig of mint**
- **1 oz. apple juice**
- **Champagne to fill**

METHOD: Put apple brandy in a tumbler with the mint and muddle the two ingredients together, slightly bruising the mint.

Add plenty of ice and then the apple juice.

SERVING SUGGESTION: Top to the brim with champagne. Taste, and say *Serendipiti!*

⸺⸺⸺

"COME QUICKLY, I AM TASTING THE STARS!"

Dom Perignon

This classic was created by Frank Meier in 1926 at the Cambon Bar, Hotel Ritz, Paris.

- Juice of ¼ lemon
- 2 oz. Pernod Fils anise (or other anise liqueur)
- Champagne

METHOD: Pour the lemon juice and the anise in a champagne coupe with a piece of ice.

SERVING SUGGESTION: Fill up with champagne and serve.

"REMEMBER GENTLEMAN, IT'S NOT JUST FRANCE WE'RE FIGHTING FOR, IT'S CHAMPAGNE!"

—*Sir Winston Churchill*

Venez jouer dehors!

COME OUT AND PLAY!

CHEZ NOUS

10 Rue Dauphine, 75006 Paris
Phone: 01 43 26 42 69
Price: *
Atmosphere: Tapas bar
http://www.cheznousparis.com/

At this newly opened natural wine bar you'll find Robin, the owner, who is passionate about his wines and who insists on never serving strange, farm-y or funky natural wines that are undrinkable for all but the mesmerized. Have him guide you and give you a tasting of two or three different glasses that are sure to surprise and really impress you. I had a Chinon from 2012 that knocked my socks off.

"CHAMPAGNE IS THE ONLY WINE THAT LEAVES A WOMAN BEAUTIFUL AFTER DRINKING IT."

—*Madame de Pompadour*

CLOWN BAR

114 rue Amelot, 75011 Paris
Phone: 01 43 55 87 35
Price: **
Atmosphere: Sultry
http://www.clown-bar-paris.fr/

Brought to you by the expert team from Saturne, one of my favorite restaurants and natural wine bars, Clown Bar offers small bites and natural wines. The tiny bistro is set in an historic site from 1917 with tiles decorating the walls picturing clowns and other artists from the nearby Cirque d'Hiver (winter circus) who used to frequent the place. Follow manager Xavier's suggestions; he won't lead you astray. Their roasted oysters from Normandy served on a broiled bed of leeks with a touch of cream and pear was unctuous and married well with the Chinon from Anjou. A romantic setting and sexy ambiance makes this a must-try spot for special occasions.

Le Baron Rouge

1 Rue Théophile Roussel, 75012 Paris

Phone: 01 43 43 14 32

Price: *

Atmosphere: Brimming with life

This wine bar near the Aligre market is a local favorite, and you can see why when you arrive around 2 p.m. on a weekend and witness the crowd spill out on the street. This might be the most convivial and friendly place in town, and with prices of wine by the glass at a mere 2 to 4 euros, your wallet won't suffer. Weekends are the most popular because, beyond the variety of assiettes on offer (sausage, hams from Corsica, rillettes, and cheese), you'll find a friendly oysterman outside who shucks for the crowd.

COMPANIE SUR VIN NATURELS

7 Rue Lobineau, 75006 Paris
Phone: 9 54 90 20 20
Price: **
Atmosphere: Elegant

One of the many feather's in ECC's cap (Experimental Cocktail Club Group), this is a grown-up wine bar offering a myriad of well-sourced and delicious wines by the glass or bottle and luscious burratta and charcuteries. Wear your heels; most of the clientele are in business attire and you'll fit in well with Dorothée Melichzon's beautifully designed décor. It's on my old street in the 6th, so I can't help but love it.

L'EBINISTE DU VIN

10 Rue Dauphine, 75006 Paris
Phone: 01 42 28 80 43
Price: **
Atmosphere: Intimate cave soirée
http://www.lebenisteduvin.fr/

L'Ebiniste du Vin and its sister L'ecaillier du Ebiniste in the 17th are wine bar extraordinaires with 500 wines on offer and more than 30 by the glass. Go early because by 8:30 p.m. this place is jam-packed with thirty- and forty-something's enjoying their wines, charcuterie, fromage, and crudités. Next door, the L'Ecailler serves fish instead of meats and is a bit smaller and slightly less crowded. Run by a husband-and-wife team, this spot is piping hot in this newly trendy part of the 17th arrondissement.

"CHAMPAGNE AND ORANGE JUICE IS A GREAT DRINK. THE ORANGE IMPROVES THE CHAMPAGNE. THE CHAMPAGNE DEFINITELY IMPROVES THE ORANGE."

—Philip, Duke of Edinburgh

— JAZZ-ERA INSPIRATIONS —

AVIATION 94

FRENCH 75 SQUARED 95

23 JUMP STREET 97

THE CHAMBER G&T 98

MISTINGUETTE 100

THE FRENCH OLD FASHIONED 104

SINGAPORE SLING 107

SWEET PEA 108

THE LAFAYETTE 109

LÉA D'ASCO 110

BRAMBLE & QUEEN 113

FORUM COCKTAIL 114

THE BASTILLE SOUR 115

THE FRENCH MANHATTAN 116

LE BON CHIC BON GENRE (BCBG) 117

LADY B 118

THE YEAR OF THE FRENCHMAN 120

THE ORIGINAL BLOODY MARY RECIPE 122

CHOCO PEAT 123

1789 125

14 JULLIET 126

FRENCH OPEN PIMM'S CUP 128

LE GRAND'S ORIGINAL DRY MARTINI 129

HIGHLAND CREAM 130

FRENCH NEGRONI 132

VERDANT MARTINI 135

PICASSO MARTINI 136

UMAMI MARTINI 137

BLOODY UMAMI 139

n researching and talking to bartenders across Paris, I learned that, in fact, cocktails have been part of French culture dating back to the early 1800s. But it is also true that the first Golden Age of cocktails in Paris occurred not coincidentally at about the same time as Prohibition began in the United States. Unemployed U.S. bartenders wandered over to Europe, ending up in the great hotels of London and Paris and beyond. Many an important cocktail was invented in Paris during this period and, not surprisingly, this was also a time that *beaucoup de* important American artists and writers descended upon the streets of Paris to seek the freedom and tolerance not found in their home country. Enjoy these Jazz Era-inspired cocktails in style.

— AVIATION —

Created in New York City in the early 1900s, this gin drink gets its purple color and flavor from a French liqueur made from real violets.

- 1½ oz. Gin (Citadelle from France or any other fine artisanal gin)
- ½ oz. fresh lemon juice
- 2 dashes Crème de Violette (Briottet or Giffard preferred)
- ½ oz. Maraschino liqueur (Luxardo preferred)

METHOD: Combine all ingredients into a cocktail shaker with ice.

Shake and strain into chilled martini glass.

SERVING SUGGESTION: Garnish with a Luxardo maraschino cherry or two!

This classic cocktail was created in 1915 at the New York Bar, the oldest bar in Paris. Harry MacElhone, the establishment's first bartender who later bought the bar, invented this one. This little drink has become re-popularized in New York and elsewhere. The name comes from a piece of French military equipment: a 75-millimeter howitzer. The reference is due to the strength of this champagne cocktail. We've added some St. Germain to French-ify the French 75 a bit more.

- 2 oz. gin
- 1 oz. lemon juice
- 1 teaspoon sugar
- 1 oz. St. Germain (or any elderflower liqueur)

- Champagne
- 2 cherries for a garnish and a lemon horseback (a very long curling twist)

METHOD: In a shaker combine the gin, lemon juice, sugar, and elderberry liqueur with cracked ice.

Strain and serve in an ice-cold coupe glass about 2/3 full, then fill with brut Champagne.

SERVING SUGGESTION: Garnish with 2 Luxardo maraschino cherries and a horse's neck lemon peel (see page 76).

This recipe serves two. Never drink the French 75 Squared alone.

BONAL

APÉRITIF - QUINA

des Montagnes de la Grande Chartreuse

ST LAURENT-DU-PONT (ISÈRE)

Bonal

QUINQUINA VIN APÉRITIF

MAISON FONDÉE EN 1865

DISTILLERIE BONAL

PRODUIT DE FRANCE

A winning recipe created by Joseph Biolatto and Yoan Bonneau for the Trophées du Bar 2012.

- 1¾ oz. Calle 23 reposado
- 1 tablespoon Bonal Quina
- 1 tablespoon *Punt e Mes Carpano* (Italian Vermouth)
- 6–8 dashes of orange bitters (preferably Fee Bros.)
- 6–8 dashes of Créole bitters by Bitter Truth

METHOD: Put all ingredients into a cocktail shaker with ice, shake, strain, and serve in a chilled martini glass with an orange twist as garnish.

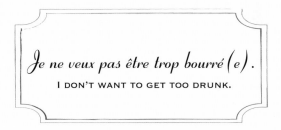

Je ne veux pas être trop bourré (e).

I DON'T WANT TO GET TOO DRUNK.

Gin and Tonics have been drunk since the nineteenth century, originally by the British in India, and have carried on throughout time in bars all over the world. "I believe the mojito has had too long of a day in Paris and it's time to replace it with a classic that is fresher and more updated," said its creator, Forest Collins. According to Ms. Collins, what makes this G&T recipe the best are the specific brands that are used here. Using what is specified will create a very different end-product than using a basic well gin and an industrial tonic.

- 1½ oz. Citadelle gin (a French gin)
- 4½ oz. Fever Tree tonic water
- Lemon zest

METHOD: Fill chilled jelly jar (or high-ball glass) with ice cubes.

Pour one part gin and three parts tonic water into the glass.

Express lemon zest over the cocktail, and drop zest into the drink.

SERVING SUGGESTION: Garnish with an edible violet.

FOREST COLLINS, INFLUENTIAL COCKTAIL BLOGGER IN PARIS (@52 MARTINIS) AND FOUNDER OF THE CHAMBER PRIVATE COCKTAIL CLUB

• • •

"SINGLE-HANDEDLY I'M TRYING TO GET PARISIANS TO START DRINKING G&TS AS THEIR GO-TO DRINK INSTEAD OF MOJITOS."

This drink's namesake was a famous French actress, singer, and dancer at the turn of the century. Her titillating act at the Moulin Rouge (and other cabarets) made her one of the highest-paid female entertainers in the world. Created by Romain at La Conserverie, Paris.

- ½ oz. honey syrup infused with horseradish
- ½ oz. pink grapefruit juice
- 2 teaspoons fresh lemon juice
- 1 oz. Lillet Blanc
- 1 oz. vodka
- Dash Jamaican jerk bitters
- Garnish with grapefruit zest

METHOD: Start with the honey syrup infused with horseradish. Make this like you would a simple syrup but instead of sugar substitute honey and then add some grated horseradish, cool, strain, and pour.

Shake all ingredients except the grapefruit zest in a cocktail shaker and strain.

SERVING SUGGESTION: Serve in a chilled martini glass with grapefruit zest floating on top.

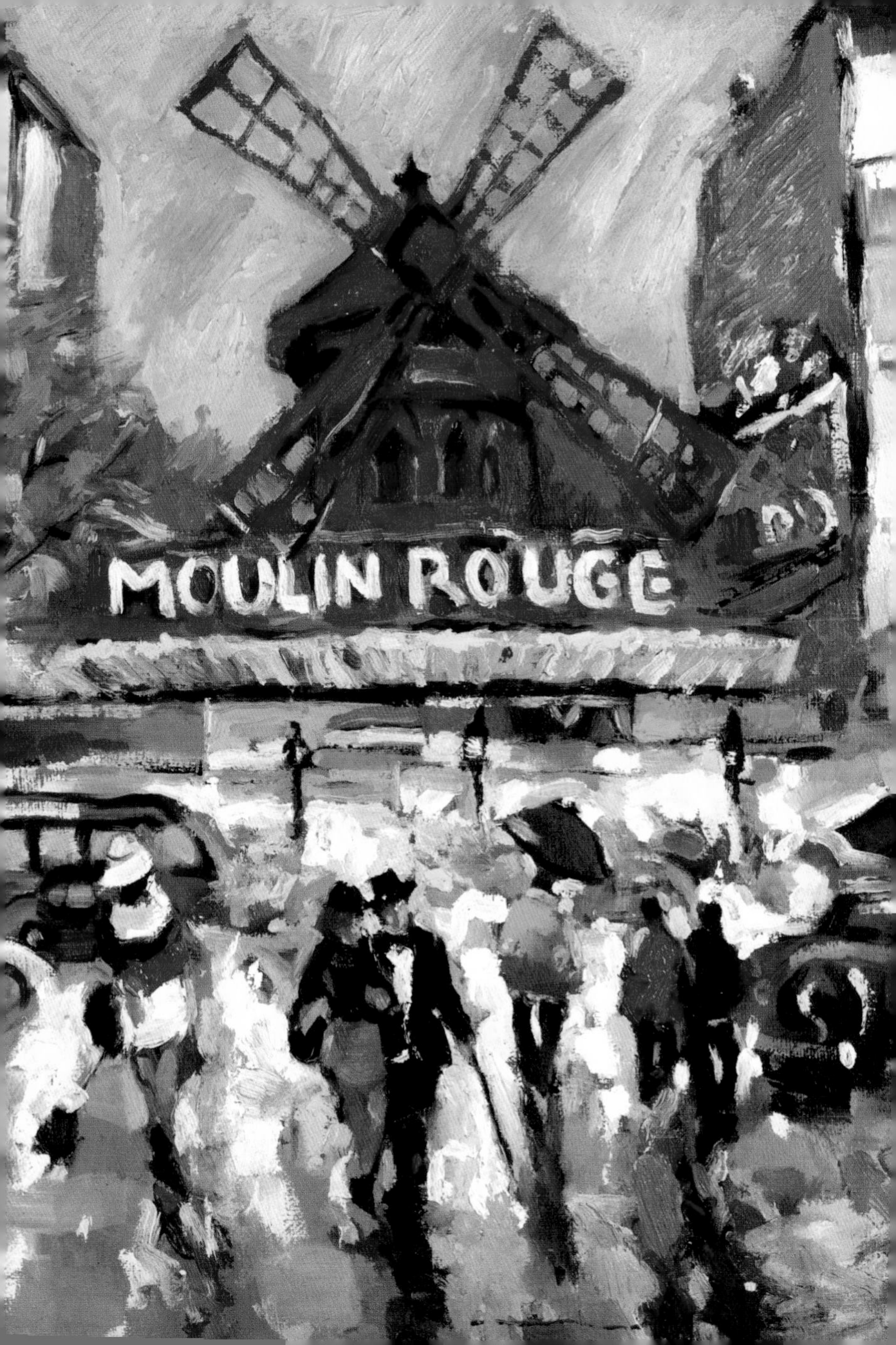
MOULIN ROUGE

Jazz Era Celebration

Ask your guests to come in their zoot suits, their fedoras, and their flapper dresses. Feathered headgear is welcome, as are long strands of pearls. In the 1920s, Paris was a hotbed of excitement and late nights were had in Montparnasse drinking in the flavors of the moment. Search for some swing and ragtime jazz on iTunes and throw in a little Piaf for good measure to put your guests in the mood.

SERVE:
French Old Fashioned (page 104) • **Sweet Pea (page 107)**
• **Singapore Slings (page 107)**

NIBBLES:
Simple classic appetizers such as devilish eggs, pork rillettes served with French bread, and devils on horseback (bacon wrapped around prunes and baked).

After a few cocktails, turn up the music and dance the night away imaging that F. Scott Fitzgerald or Gertrude Stein might just walk in the door any minute.

— THE FRENCH OLD FASHIONED —

The Old Fashioned was perhaps the very first cocktail. It was simple and considered a cure of sorts, normally to be taken in the morning after having too much the night before. Now I enjoy an Old Fashioned, but never ever during an hour that ends in a.m. Here's a version that lightens it up a bit with club soda, to be served in the evening.

- 2 oz. Bastille Whisky (or favorite whisky)
- 4 dashes Angostura bitters
- 1 teaspoon sugar (or 2 sugar cubes)
- 1 splash club soda
- 1 orange wheel
- 1 maraschino cherry

METHOD: Combine the whisky, bitters, sugar, and soda, and serve in a rocks glass garnished with a cherry and orange wheel.

The Singapore Sling was first created in Singapore at the Raffles hotel around 1915. It's a pleasure to try this less-sweet version at the Raffles-owned, Phillippe Starck–designed bar at Le Royal Monceau, Paris (see page 36).

- 1 oz. gin
- 1¾ tablespoons of cherry brandy
- 2 teaspoons Cointreau (or your preferred triple sec)
- 3 teaspoons Bénédictine
- A dash of grenadine
- 1⅓ tablespoons lime juice
- 1 oz. pineapple juice
- Soda water to fill

METHOD: Put all the ingredients except the soda into the shaker with ice. Shake vigorously and serve in a high-ball glass with ice cubes and top up with soda water.

SERVING SUGGESTION: Garnish with three maraschino cherries and a slice of lemon.

à Votre Santé!

TO YOUR HEATH!

(THIS IS YOUR MOST STANDARD
PHRASE TO USE WHEN TOASTING;
IT CAN BE SHORTENED
TO À LA VOTRE OR JUST SANTÉ).

— SWEET PEA —

This cocktail was invented for composer Cole Porter, who was a regular at the Hemingway bar, Ritz Hotel, Paris.

- 3 oz. anise liqueur (such as Pernod)
- 1 oz. lemon juice
- Tonic to fill

METHOD: Pour the anise and lemon directly into a high-ball glass with ice and fill with a good tonic.

―――――

"I LOVE PARIS IN THE
SUMMER, WHEN IT SIZZLES."

Cole Porter

Lafayette was a major French figure who helped America win its independence. He was a hero to the French and Americans alike, hence the inclusion of bourbon, a completely American liquor.

• 1¾ oz. bourbon

• ¾ oz. lemon juice

• 1¼ oz. grapefruit juice

• ¾ oz. Mandarin liqueur

METHOD: Shake liquid ingredients with ice and 5 mint leaves (crushed) in your cocktail shaker.

Strain and serve in a high-ball glass with a few cubes of ice.

SERVING SUGGESTION: Garnish with a mint stalk.

"SOMETHING ABOUT GLAMOUR INTERESTED ME.
ALL MY SCHOOLBOOKS HAD DRAWINGS OF WOMEN ON
TERRACES WITH A COCKTAIL AND A CIGARETTE."

—*Bill Blass*

— LÉA D'ASCO —

Here we have an English and French combo, which is what its creator Matthew Long is: a Londoner who is very much at home behind the bar at Lulu White in Paris. He named this cocktail after a singer from the Folies Bergère.

- ½ oz. Beefeater Gin
- 1 oz. Lillet Blanc
- 1 tablespoon Armorik Classic Whisky from Brittany
- A little bit less than a tablespoon of Pernod Absinthe
- Orange zest for garnish

METHOD: Stir all liquid ingredients above together for 20 seconds.

SERVING SUGGESTION: Strain into a chilled martini glass and garnish with orange zest.

> Absinthe is an alcoholic substance infused with wormwood. Pernod is one of the oldest producers. Absinthe was banned in 1912 in the United States due to a myth that is caused hallucinations. The ban was lifted in 2007. Absinthe is now made in Switzerland (where it originated), France, Germany, the Czech Republic, and the States.

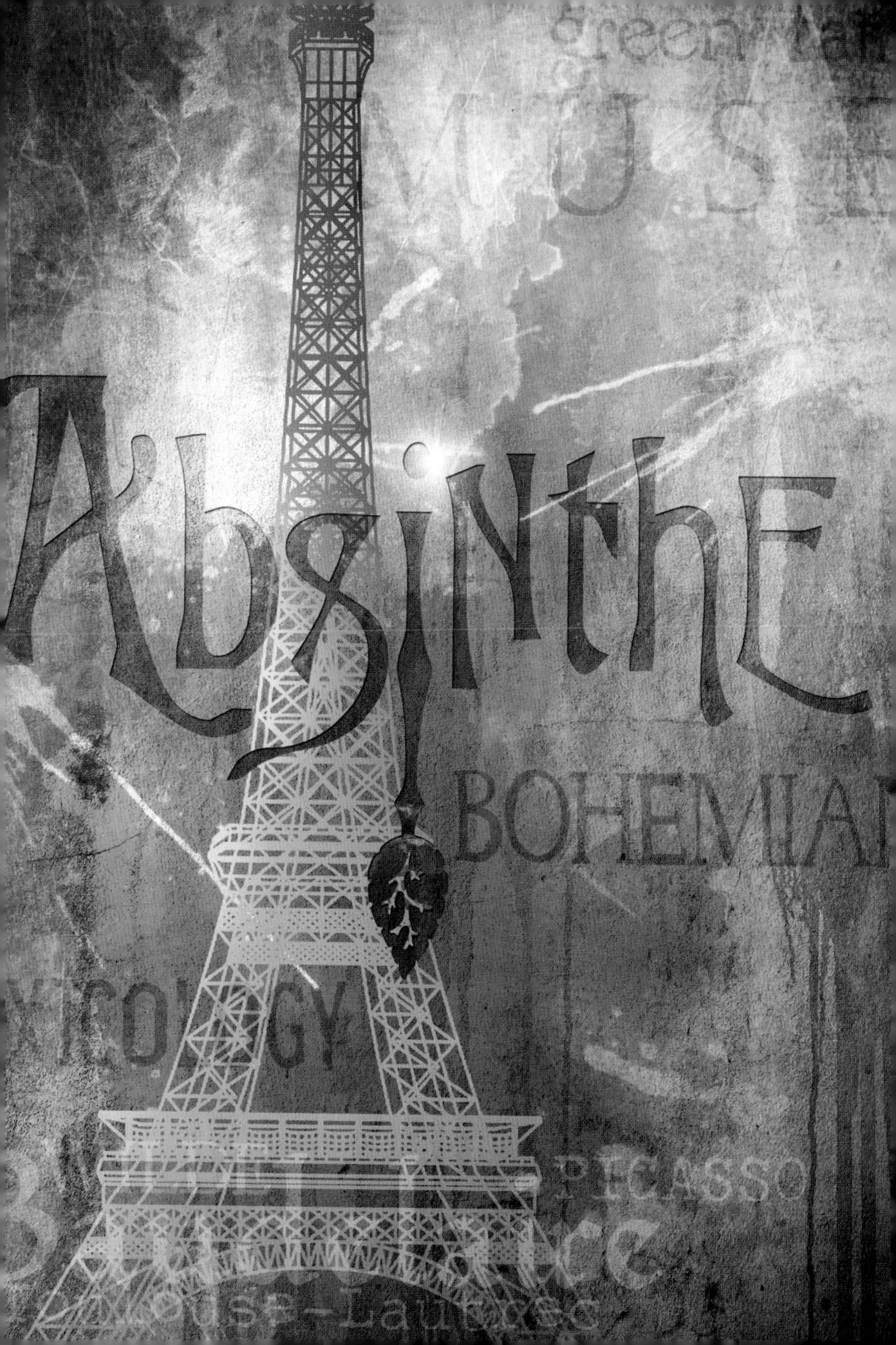
green
Absinthe
PICASSO

This lovely drink might be considered a ladies' cocktail, but don't tell the guys who will also love it! Created by Yann Daniel at the Park Hyatt Vendome, Paris.

- ½ oz. gin (they use Beefeater at the Vendome)
- ½ oz. fresh lemon juice
- ½ oz. sugar cane syrup
- 1 teaspoon ylang ylang water
- Egg white
- Champagne to top
- 1 tablespoon blackberry liqueur

METHOD: Pour the gin, lemon juice, syrup, and ylang ylang water in the shaker. Shake it well with a little bit of egg white to obtain a frothy mixture.

Strain the cocktail into a cold martini or coupe glass and top with champagne adding the blackberry liqueur at the very end.

SERVING SUGGESTION: Garnish the cocktail with a lemongrass loop and 3 fresh blackberries on a bamboo stick.

If you can't find ylang ylang water, substitute jasmine water made by Fee Brothers, among other companies.

This is the signature cocktail of the 85-year-old bar in Paris's 8th arrondissement, created in 1929 as their version of a gin martini.

- **1½ oz. gin**
- **2 teaspoons Noilly Prat Vermouth**
- **4–5 drops Grand Marnier**

METHOD: Stir in a large glass with ice, strain, and pour into a frozen martini glass.

SERVING SUGGESTION: Garnish with an orange twist.

> I started work on this book with the belief that I did not like gin. I had refused to budge on this position for twenty years. But, after trying gin cocktails all over Paris, in particular the new Pink Peppercorn Gin distilled in France, I changed my mind entirely. If you are still in the other camp, you can always substitute vodka for gin in these recipes but I would urge you to take a fresh look at gin—you might be pleasantly surprised.

The Whisky Sour is a quintessential classic, but the twist here is using not only a French-made whisky but adding the floral notes of St. Germain liqueur, also crafted in France.

- **2 oz. Bastille Whisky**
- **¾ oz. St. Germain liqueur (or any elderflower liqueur)**
- **Juice of 3/4 fresh lemon**
- **One egg white**

METHOD: Put all ingredients together in a cocktail shaker with ice.

SERVING SUGGESTION: Serve chilled and frothy in a rocks glass with some ice.

"AYE, BUT TODAY'S RAIN IS TOMORROW'S WHISKY."

—*Scottish proverb*

— THE FRENCH MANHATTAN —

This is my husband's go-to drink in the winter, French-ified by the addition of whisky made in France.

- 2½ oz. Bastille Whisky
- ¼ oz. sweet vermouth
- 1 dash Angostura bitters

METHOD: Shake the liquid ingredients with ice and strain. Serve chilled in a martini class.

SERVING SUGGESTION: Garnish with an orange peel twist and a cherry.

Who are the BCBG crowd anyway? These are your French preppies; you'll find them in the 16th and 7th arrondissements in Paris. They can be easily spotted wearing cashmere sweaters in bright colors wrapped around their shoulders. But even if this type doesn't appeal to you, this drink will.

- **Muddled fresh rosemary, orange zest, and agave nectar**
- **2 oz. Bastille Whisky**

- **2 oz. Domaine de Canton (or any ginger liqueur)**
- **1 oz. white wine**
- **2 oz. apple cider**
- **Splash of fresh lemon juice**

METHOD: Muddle your herbs, orange zest, and agave nectar; add the rest of the ingredients and shake with ice. Strain, and serve on the rocks in a highball glass.

SERVING SUGGESTION: Garnish with a sprig of rosemary.

> Domaine de Canton is a ginger liqueur produced in Jarnac, France using Cognac and baby Chinese ginger, among other ingredients.

— LADY B —

If you are trying to introduce a lady to whisky, first of all you must use Brenne, which is aged in cognac barrels. It's also 100 percent smoother than most whisky I've tasted. With these two additions, you can turn a whisky-hater into a whisky-lover in one cocktail.

- 2 oz. Brenne Whisky
- 2 oz. soda water
- 2 oz. Lillet

METHOD: Stir the whisky and Lillet together with ice and strain over ice into a rocks glass. Top with soda water.

SERVING SUGGESTION: Garnish with an orange peel.

LILLET

Established in 1872

LILLET A PODENSAC-GIRON

Apéritif de France

PRODUCED AND BOTTLED BY :

LILLET

Podensac - Gironde - France

PRODUCT OF FRANCE

SERVE WELL CHILLED

I adore the title of this drink, and knowing it comes from a former American ballerina who now makes Brenne Whisky in the cognac region of France just makes it all the merrier.

- **2 oz. Brenne Whisky**
- **½ oz. agave nectar (or simple syrup)**
- **¾ oz. fresh lime juice**

- **3 dashes celery bitters**
- **1 teaspoon Sorel (or any hibiscus liqueur)**

METHOD: Shake all ingredients except the hibiscus liqueur with ice and strain into a chilled coupe glass.

Float a teaspoon of Sorel or other hibiscus liqueur on top.

> Sorel is a brand of hibiscus liqueur made by the company Jack from Brooklyn. But several companies make hibiscus liqueurs.

HARRY'S NEW YORK BAR

5 Daunou Street, 75002 Paris
Phone: 01 42 61 71 14
Price: **
Atmosphere: Classic New York style
http://www.harrysbar.fr/

An institution in the 2nd arrondissement inhabiting the same spot since 1911, this New York Bar was actually moved to Paris over 100 years ago and then later bought by its first bartender named Harry. A Frenchman named Ferdinand Petiot (Pete by the expats) invented the Bloody Mary here in 1921, only to later bring it to New York and the St. Regis Hotel. This place is all about class, great service, and incredibly smooth classic cocktails. The ambiance upstairs and down is heaven, exactly what a New York–style bar should look and feel like. There's jazz downstairs on the weekends, but buyer beware: there's no nonsense around here—Harry's serves absolutely no wine and no coffee— you are coming here to drink, baby!

Created by Harry's New York Bar in 1921 by bartender Ferdinand "Pete" Petiot to help a regular's hangover, what's noticeable here is what isn't included in later recipes. There's no lime (just lemon), no celery salt, no Tabasco sauce, and no horseradish.

- Salt, cayenne pepper, and black pepper to taste
- 6 dashes of Worstershire sauce
- Juice of ½ a lemon
- 2 oz. vodka
- 2 oz. tomato juice

METHOD: Create this in the glass starting with 4 dashes of salt, 2 of cayenne, and 2 dashed of black pepper.

Add the Worstershire, lemon, vodka, and finally the tomato juice.

> Be sure to use ground not cracked black pepper and do not add celery salt! Originally there was no garnish, and to this day at Harry's you won't get a wedge of lemon, or a celery stick, or, God forbid, a pickle! They do add Tabasco sauce now, so feel free to add a dash or two to this if you prefer, but why not give it a sip first?

f you like chocolate, you'll love this one! Here's another drink that can convert a non-whisky lover into one. I like to substitute this instead of dessert. Created at Harry's Bar, Paris.

- ½ oz. dark chocolate liqueur (Monin brand is preferred)
- ¾ oz. Kahlua
- 1¼ oz. Stolichnaya Hot Vodka (or any spicy vodka)
- ¾ oz. Peat Monster Whisky

METHOD: Stir all ingredients in a cocktail glass with ice, strain, and serve in a martini glass, no garnish needed.

ALAIN, CHEF DU BAR AT HARRY'S NEW YORK BAR

• • •

"MORE AND MORE PEOPLE ARE GOING OUT FOR COCKTAILS, AND HERE WE SERVE THEM IN TRADITIONAL WHITE COATS SINCE 1911. THE UNIFORM IS IMPORTANT: IT SHOWS THAT OUR CUSTOMER IS NUMBER ONE."

1789 was the year of the storming of the Bastille, the first French revolution (there were a few, in fact). Created by Harry's Bar, Paris.

- ½ oz. **Bonal Quina (or your preferred apéritif white wine)**
- ½ oz. **Lillet**
- 1 ⅓ oz. **Bastille Whisky**

METHOD: In a mixing glass add all three ingredients with ice cubes, stir, strain, and serve in a chilled martini glass.

SERVING SUGGESTION: Rim just half the martini glass with Tabasco salt.

Bonal Quina and Lillet are both French apéritif wines.

Harry's New York Bar created this as a cocktail to complement the first French whisky they ever served: Bastille (hence the patriotic name).

- 4 wedges of lime
- 2 oz. Bastille Whisky
- ½ tablespoon fig syrup (Monin makes a good one)
- Ginger beer to top

METHOD: Squeeze the lime into a tumbler full of ice, and add whisky and the fig syrup (add less than the allotted amount if you like your drink less sweet).

Top off with ginger beer (Fever Tree recommended). Ahhh, refreshing!

> If you'd prefer to make your own fig syrup rather than buying it, take a dozen figs (trimming off tops and bottoms) and add them to your simple syrup as you heat it up. Mash the figs as the water simmers. Take off stove after about 5–10 minutes or once sugar has dissolved; let sit to macerate fully for about 20–30 minutes. Strain and use or place in refrigerator for up to two weeks.

HEMINGWAY BAR AT THE RITZ BAR

15 Place Vendome, 75001 Paris
Phone: 01 43 16 30 30
Price: ***
Atmosphere: Stepping back in time
http://www.ritzparis.com/

This bar holds a critical place in the history of Paris cocktail culture. *Chef du bar* Colin Peter Field was named by *Forbes* as the greatest bartender in the world. If you read his book *Bar Hemingway,* you might agree. His predecessor Frank Meier, who served Ernest Hemingway among other elites, was also enormously important in developing the cocktails we still drink today. The Sidecar was invented by Frank, but I'd suggest trying the Ritz's Pimm's Cup in the summer (after all, the bartender is British). Or make yourself a French-ified version, a French Open Pimm's Cup (page 128).

LE GRAND HOTEL

2 Rue Scribe, 75009 Paris
Phone: 01 40 07 32 32
Price: ***
Atmosphere: Historic and grand
http://www.ihg.com/intercontinental/hotels/gb/en/paris/parhb/hoteldetail

It was a grand pleasure to sip their own version of the classic gin martini created by Frank Newman in 1904 in this historic bar that's been at this very location since the hotel was created by Napoleon III. While my go-to martini is made with vodka, olives, and onions, it was exciting to try Le Grand's Original Dry Martini (page 129) with Tanqueray gin, Noilly Prat Vermouth, orange bitters, and a Luxardo maraschino cherry. This bar should be your go-to place for a drink before or after attending the Opera Garnier next door.

"HERE'S TO ALCOHOL, THE ROSE COLORED GLASSES OF LIFE."

F. Scott Fitzgerald, The Beautiful and Damned

The Pimm's Cup is the most English of cocktails invented in the UK is popular at Wimbledon, polo, and cricket matches. Here we French-ify it a bit with Lorina French sparkling lemonade. Make a pitcher for a garden party or an afternoon watching the French Open on the telly.

- 2 cups Pimm's No. 1
- 4 cups Lorina French Sparkling Lemonade
- 1 English cucumber sliced lengthwise thinly such that everyone can get a slice in their drink
- Lemons and limes cut into thin rounds
- 1 green apple sliced in small edible chunks
- 8 sprigs of mint crushed

METHOD: Begin with a pitcher full of ice and add your fruit, cucumber, and mint stirring a bit to bruise the mint.

Add the Pimm's and the Lorina. Chill before serving.

SERVING SUGGESTION: Make sure everyone gets some citrus, apple and mint in their glass as well as more ice.

The "Original Dry Martini," as it was named and created by Frank Newman at the Le Grand hotel bar, is a very different and later version than the classic gin martini that was originally created in New York City. So we can call this the Parisian version, and it is quite tasty although it is anything but dry considering how much vermouth is involved.

- 1¼ oz. Noilly Prat dry vermouth
- 1¼ Tanqueray gin
- 2 dashes of bitter orange

METHOD: Put the ingredients in a mixing glass full of ice and serve in a chilled martini glass without ice cubes.

SERVING SUGGESTION: Garnish with a Luxardo maraschino cherry or a basic cocktail cherry.

REGARDING A MARTINI:

"I HAD NEVER TASTED ANYTHING SO COOL AND CLEAN. ...
THEY MADE ME FEEL CIVILIZED."

—Ernest Hemingway, in Farewell to Arms

This is a coffee/choco after-dinner drink with whisky. Colin from Bar Hemingway has been perfecting it for years. I think he's got it right!

- 1 oz. Grant's Blended Scotch Whisky
- 2 oz. coffee liqueur
- 2 oz. crème de cacao bean liqueur
- 1 oz. espresso coffee
- 4 oz. crème fraiche

METHOD: Pour all ingredients into a shaker filled with ice.

SERVING SUGGESTION: Serve in a Martini glass. Garnish with a little chocolate powder.

COLIN PETER FIELD, HEAD BARTENDER AT THE RITZ AND AUTHOR OF BAR HEMINGWAY

• • •

"REGULARS ALWAYS COME ALONE AND I OFTEN INTRODUCE WHOMEVER IS THERE TO EACH OTHER UNLESS I NOTICE THAT THEY WANT TO BE ALONE. A BARTENDER MUST BE A SALESMAN AND A HOST."

Rosebud

11 B Rue Delambre, 75014 Paris, France
Phone: 01 43 35 38 54
Price: **
Atmosphere: 60s jazz

Rosebud is an outrageously charming bar in the 14th arrondissement with waiters in white coats and palm trees adding to the atmosphere. This circa 1962 bar is "Mad Men"-meets-Paris where the martini glasses are small, just as they were back in the day, and the martini's bone dry. Only vintage cocktails are on offer such as negronis, fizzes, Collins, and the like. With an older, non-hipster crowd and jazz playing on the speakers, this place is truly my cup of tea, so much so that when I visited I actually ordered a second martini, something I've learned many times that I cannot, should not, and will *never* do again. I'm writing it on the blackboard: *one martini is perfect, two is too much. One martini...*

(v)

A classic with a French touch.

- 1½ oz. gin
- 1 oz. Suze

- 1 oz. sweet vermouth (such as the French-made Dolin or Noilly Pratt)
- Orange twist

METHOD: Add the liquid ingredients in the order given in a tall glass and serve on ice with an orange twist.

à Boire ou je tue le chien!

BRING ME SOMETHING TO DRINK OR I'LL KILL THE DOG

(A COLLOQUIALISM).

At L'Apicius, Valentin creates bespoke cocktails. He'll ask you what you are in the mood for; you don't have to tell him much and he'll come up with something spectacular. This is what I asked for one night at their gorgeous bar in Paris, I feel this is my own new version of a martini.

- 4 green shiso cress
- 2 borage cress
- Kona Sansho (Japanese pepper)
- 2 oz. London dry gin (or your favorite gin)
- 2 dashes Noilly prat dry vermouth

METHOD: In a mixing glass, put green shiso, borage, and a pinch of Kona Sansho.

Add the gin and the Noilly prat and mix it strongly with a lot of ice.

Double strain in a very cold martini glass.

SERVING SUGGESTION: Decorate with a green shiso, purple shiso, and borage cress leaves.

VARIATION: I make this drink with Dragon Bleu Vodka instead of gin.

To make this particularly elegant and exotic martini as Valentin does in Paris, you'll want to visit an Asian market for some of the more unusual products such as the Japanese pepper, which comes in a bottle (Kona Sancho), and the shiso leaves. The borage cress are the first sprout leaves of a borage plant and taste like cucumber. If you can't find the cress, substitute a thin slice of a Japanese or European cucumber.

This is a beautiful take on the classic martini via Colin Peter Field from Bar Hemingway at the Ritz. I'll let you discern the Cubist reference.

- **Noilly Pratt Vermouth ice cube**
- **Gin or vodka**

METHOD: Freeze 1 ice cube with Noilly Pratt Vermouth.

Pour your favorite gin or vodka into a frozen martini glass and add the vermouth ice cube.

SERVING SUGGESTION: Garnish as you like with olives or lemon rind twist.

"HAPPINESS IS... FINDING TWO OLIVES IN YOUR MARTINI WHEN YOU'RE HUNGRY."

—Johnny Carson

— UMAMI MARTINI —

Umami is an entirely new class of liquor. Made in the Cognac region of France by Audemus Spirits, the idea was to come up with a savory liquor to use in savory drinks. Umami uses cornichons as well as over twenty other secret spices to flavor this liquor like the fifth taste, umami. So far it's available in France and the UK. If you can get your hands on it, you've got to try the Umami Martini.

- **White vermouth for rinsing a frozen glass**
- **2 oz. Umami**

METHOD: Rinse a frozen martini glass with ice and white vermouth and discard both.

Pour 2 oz. Umami into the glass.

SERVING SUGGESTION: Serve with an olive or two!

"A MAN MUST DEFEND HIS HOME, HIS WIFE, HIS CHILDREN, AND HIS MARTINI."

—*Jackie Gleason*

And then you'll want to bring that fifth taste to the classic Bloody Mary.

- 1½ oz. umami
- ¾ cup of tomato juice
- 2 dashes of Worstershire sauce
- 1 dash (or more as desired) or Tabasco
- 1 dash of celery bitter
- Salt and pepper to taste

METHOD: Create this drink in your rocks glass with ice starting with the flavorings and then adding the Umami and then the tomato juice.

SERVING SUGGESTION: Stir and garnish with a lemon peel, a celery stick, a pickled green been, several olives or all of the above.

Allons-y pour prendre un apéro.

LET'S GO FOR A DRINK
(AN APERITIF).

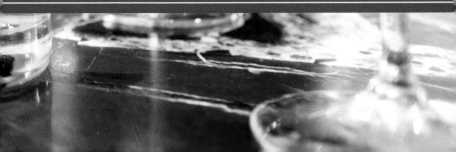

CASUAL AND CREATIVE COCKTAILS —

THE SOIRÉE 144

CERISE SOIR 145

L'ORANGE PASSION 148

FRENCH MARTINI DE NANCY 150

PPR 151

JENNIFER'S SLIPPER 152

THE LAST CALL 153

don't know about you, but I have been in a cocktail rut before. A simple cure for this issue is to step out of your comfort zone. Try an entirely new cocktail from this book to serve to your guests, be they drop-by friends or proper party guests. Perk up a no-plans Friday night creating something entirely new and French-inspired to share with your love. With an open mind and some good products, you'll be surprised at what you can come up with.

Not every night sipping cocktails has to be grand; the new cool-kids casualness that grew up in Brooklyn means that, even when you are not watching your wallet, dive bars—and the drinks those barmen serve—can be a welcome break from having to get your heels and your bowties on. A little down and dirty is good for us all.

> *Il n'y a qu'un bonheur dans la vie, c'est d'aimer et d'être aimé.*
>
> **THERE IS ONLY ONE HAPPINESS IN LIFE: TO LOVE AND BE LOVED.**
> (FROM CORRESPONDENCE À LINA CALMATTA BY GEORGES SAND)

Whose I was asked to speak about Paris Cocktails for a fête that a friend (Patricia Laplante-Collins) was hosting in Paris, I decided to make three cocktails for the group. This was the most successful of them all.

- 2 oz. Pink Pepper Gin by Audemus

- 1 oz. Pamplemousse Rose liqueur (Combier, Cartron & Briottet all make nice versions)
- Juice of ½ a lemon

METHOD: Stir over ice, pour into a chilled coupe glass, and serve with a lemon twist and several pink peppercorns floating.

VARIATION: If you prefer a less strong drink, add champagne or sparkling water and serve over ice in a tall glass.

> If you can't find the pink peppercorn flavored gin by Audemus, try Big Gin by Captive Spirits made in Seattle or Cardinal Gin made by Southern Artisan spirits of North Carolina.

Created by my friend Jennifer at a Friday night party in Paris, this is a lovely way to enjoy the orange shrub liquor made in Martinique with rum and orange peel.

- 1 teaspoon simple syrup
- Squeeze of a lemon wedge
- 1 teaspoon Griottines juice (cherries in kirsch)
- 1 oz. shrub liquor made in Martinique (made with rum and orange peel)

METHOD: Shake with ice all ingredients save the cherries, strain, and serve in a cold Nick and Nora glass.

SERVING SUGGESTION: Garnish with 2 Griottine cherries (or substitute your favorite cocktail cherries).

A Nick and Nora glass, or a sherry glass, is like a mini-martini glass but with a curve at the bottom instead of a point.

—Make-Your-Own Cocktail Friday—

This is a casual party; tell your guests to come dressed comfortably. Print out a selection of five to seven of the most intriguing cocktails that you find in this book. Put each recipe (perhaps laminated) in front of a selection of its ingredients at various stations around a large table. Ask everyone to make their own cocktails according to the recipes; tell folks to share tastings to figure out who likes what best.

Lay out a charcuterie *assiette* with a selection of French *fromage*, sausages, pâtés, and Basque hams like jambon de Bayonne. Offer a

spicy espelette pepper jelly alongside some of the harder Spanish or Basque-style cheeses. Include some cherry tomatoes (Parisians are crazy for them!) and French olives, not forgetting a tiny vessel to discard the pits. A big basket of sliced French baguette is *de rigeur*.

For cocktail round two, ask your guests to play around with the ingredients to create their own bespoke concoction.

For the actual meal, serve your favorite soup recipe with more crusty French bread and a bottle or two of Côtes du Rhône.

Follow up the next day by emailing all of your guests the recipes to keep.

This drink was concocted during a drink-making experiment chez moi. It's a French version of a Tequila Sunrise, I imagine.

- 1 oz. Teqilla
- ½ oz. Lillet
- ½ oz. Cointreau (or your preferred triple sec)

- Orange juice
- Passion fruit juice
- Lime juice

METHOD: Put the alcohol ingredients above in your cocktail shaker and then add 1 part orange juice and 1 part passion fruit juice (equaling no more than as much as the liquor in the glass for a strong drink and ⅔ to ⅓ liquor for a weaker drink).

Add a healthy squeeze of lime. Shake it up well, strain and serve in a high-ball glass on the rock.

SERVING SUGGESTION: Garnish with a lime wedge and lemon peel.

One night in Paris, I had a bunch of girls over to make French versions of classic cocktails (hey, a gal can't drink alone, right?) and my friend Nancy, who flew all the way from New York, helped massage this less sweet version of the classic, so she deserves some props.

- ½ oz. Pamplemousse Rose liqueur
- 1½ oz. Ciroc vodka (or your favorite vodka)
- A good squeeze of lemon
- 2 oz. grapefruit juice
- Grapefruit zest

METHOD: Put the liquid ingredients in your cocktail shaker with ice, shake, and strain.

SERVING SUGGESTION: Serve in a martini glass with grapefruit zest sprinkled on top.

C

reated by my amazing team of girlfriends in Paris, with special input from my friend Dana.

- 2½ oz. rum
- ¾ oz. Pamplemousse Rose liqueur
- ¾ oz. lemon juice
- 1 barspoon of Luxardo cherry liqueur
- 3 dashes of Peychaud bitters

METHOD: Mix liquid ingredients. Add crushed ice and stir well.

SERVING SUGGESTION: Garnish with grapefruit peel zest and a maraschino cherry.

On peut avoir la même chose, s'il vous plaît ?

ANOTHER ROUND PLEASE!

This recipe comes from the winner of a cocktail contest that we had on the Girls' Guide to Paris Facebook page, and Jennifer won! Interestingly I didn't tell them that they had to use French ingredients, but Midori is actually manufactured in France for all of Europe (though it starts with special melons from Japan).

- 1 oz. shot of tequila
- ½ oz. Midori
- 2 oz. shot sour mix (see recipe sidebar)

METHOD: Combine liquid ingredients and shake with crushed ice. Strain, pour, and serve in a frozen martini glass.

SERVING SUGGESTION: Garnish with two maraschino cherries.

MAKE YOUR OWN SOUR MIX: Homemade sour mix is much tastier than anything store bought. All you need is: 1 cup sugar, 1 cup water, 2 cups fresh lime and lemon juice strained (no pulp). Combine water and sugar and simmer until the sugar dissolves. Turn the heat down to simmer and add your citrus juice. Remove from the fire and let the mixture sit before straining into a bottle. Store in an airtight bottle in the fridge for up to two weeks. Enjoy!

Not a bad idea to order this up at home as your last call before tucking into bed. Easy to make and smooth on the tongue.

• **2 oz. Brenne Whisky**

• **1 oz. Sorel (Hibiscus Liqueur)**

METHOD: Shake the two ingredients with ice and strain into a chilled coupe glass.

SERVING SUGGESTION: Garnish with a hibiscus flower.

LA FOLIE EN TÊTE

33 Rue de La Butte aux Cailles, 75013 Paris
Phone: 01 45 80 65 99
Price: *
Atmosphere: Old school artistic
http://lafolieentete.wix.com/lesite

Looking for a cheap drink in the 13th arrondissement? Then this is your place, especially during happy hour from 5 to 8 p.m. The atmosphere has a relaxed artsy feel, with old school chairs and wooden instruments adorning the walls.

CHARLOTTE GALITZINE, OWNER AND BARTENDER AT LE CHARLIE

• • •

"I WANTED TO CREATE A NEIGHBORHOOD BAR WITH CHEAP BUT GOOD BEER AND COCKTAILS WHERE IT WAS EASY FOR A YOUNG PERSON TO BE ABLE TO BUY A ROUND OF DRINKS FOR THEIR FRIENDS. MY FRIEND WHO FOUND THE VESPA ON THE WALL HAS FREE DRINKS FOR LIFE HERE!"

Le Charlie

29 Rue de Cotte, 75012 Paris
Phone: 01 53 33 02 67
Price: *
Atmosphere: Hipster dive

At the helm is a bartender by the name of Charlotte, who welcomes visitors warmly at her tiny little bar in the Bastille neighborhood. The atmosphere is shabby-hipster dive bar chic, and there's a darling little cave area downstairs where you and your friends can drink all night long. The prices are pleasing.

Les Idiots

115 Boulevard de Ménilmontant, 75011 Paris
Phone: 06 37 61 85 87
Price: *
Atmosphere: Casual Parisian dive

This is a type of place that I come to Paris for. It's tiny and bohemian with affordable drinks, a cool crowd, and very friendly service, yet no tourists anywhere to be found. I only wish it was walking distance from my apartment.

Les Pères Populaires

46 rue de Buzenval, 75020 Paris
Phone: 01 43 48 49 22
Price: *
Atmosphere: Penny-pinching grunge

If you are looking for the quintessential grunge hipster in Paris, look no further. You'll find hipsters here in droves drinking cheap wine at this unassuming hotspot in the 20th arrondissement. All the wines by the glass come from boxes, but the red Chinon, for a mere 3.5 euros, is quite good. You can order a sandwich or a charcuterie plate and be happy drinking beers or a basic mojito all night long and leave with money left in your pocket.

— JOYEUSE HOLIDAYS —

PISTE VERTE 160

CHARTREUSE MULE 161

VIN CHAUD 164

CRANBERRY SPARKLER 165

BRENNE CHAI TODDY 166

EDUCATION SENTIMENTALE 168

POMEGRANATE MARGARITA 169

It's truly sublime to spend the holiday season in Paris. One can soak up the spectacle that is Paris and enjoy the season without all the crass commercialization that we now find elsewhere. If you can't make it this year, create your own little French fête at home. *Bonne Année!*

— PISTE VERTE —

Named after the bunny slope, this winter drink made with pine liqueur is a fresh take on *hiver* by Romain at La Conserverie, Paris.

- 2 teaspoons honey syrup (see instructions below)
- 1 oz. Mamont Vodka
- 1 oz. Liqueur de Sapin Dolin
- 1 oz. fresh clementine juice
- ½ oz. fresh lemon juice

METHOD: Honey syrup is made just like simple syrup but using honey instead of sugar. Heat 1 cup of honey with 1 cup of water until the honey is incorporated and dissolved, let cool, and use. Store the remainder in the fridge for up to 2 weeks.

Shake all ingredients with ice in a cocktail shaker, strain, and serve garnished with mint leaves in a wine glass.

> Sapin liqueur is made in France by a variety of distillers such as Dolin and Les Fils d'Emile Perot.

A take on the Mule using green Chartreuse still made by the Carthusian monks and thought to be since its inception in the 1600s the elixir of long life. Cheers!

- 1 oz. Chartreuse Verte
- 2 teaspoons fresh lemon juice
- A splash of ginger beer

METHOD: Pour Chartreuse and lemon juice in a rocks glass over ice.

Top off with a splash of ginger beer.

Boire comme un trou

A COLLOQUIAL PHRASE
MEANING TO DRINK A LOT
(LITERALLY, DRINK LIKE
YOU HAVE A HOLE TO FILL)

Joyeuse Noel Fête

This fête should begin after dinner around 8:30 p.m. because dessert is the concept. Set your iTunes or radio to a playlist of traditional Christmas carols interspersed with some French ones such as those found on the CD "Chants de Noel" (French Christmas Songs) by Hélène Baillargeon.

Offer a selection of French Holiday cocktails such as Vin Chaud (page 164), the Cranberry Sparkler (page 165), and the Brenne Chai Toddy (page 166).

Bring a white elephant gift (something lying around your house that is new and nice but you don't use or care for anymore). You know the drill!

Do a French holiday dessert exchange, similar to a cookie exchange. Ask each guest or couple to bring their favorite French homemade dessert (extra busy souls can buy something spectacular and French at a nearby bakery).

The best type of things to bring to an exchange are items that are small and number at least twenty-five to fifty depending on the number of guests invited. Items such as Cognac truffles, Madeleines, mini-chocolate fondants, macarons, cling-film wrapped slices of Buche de Noel, squares of Nougat blanc, Callissons, Pain des Epices (spicy French Hazelnut Christmas bread), and chocolate-covered orange rind slices.

Supply some nice vintage cookie tins or decorate boxes with tissue. Lay out all of the wares on a table. Nibbling is allowed. Then as people are leaving, have them take several from each offering so that everyone goes home with a nice selection of all of the various desserts. This is the spirit of Christmas: share and share alike.

— VIN CHAUD —

This classic hot mulled red wine is served in most Parisian bars and cafés all winter long. It will warm you up fast!

- 1 bottle inexpensive red wine (Cote du Rhone or Bordeaux preferred)
- 1 star anise
- 2 slices fresh ginger (or sugared ginger)
- 3 cloves
- 2 cardamom pods
- 1 tablespoon of orange and lemon zest
- ½ cup honey
- ½ cup cognac, pear eau de vie, or Calvados (depending on what you like)

METHOD: Put all ingredients except the cognac into a nonreactive pan with spices, and heat until simmering.

Add the cognac or eau de vie at the end, after you've taken the hot liquid off the fire.

SERVING SUGGESTION: Serve in a heat-resistant glass mug with a cinnamon stick.

This makes the perfect holiday cocktail.

• ½ oz. Cranberry Liqueur by Edmond Briottet

• 2 teaspoon of Cocchi Americano Rosa (or sweet vermouth)

• 2 oz. champagne (or crémant)

METHOD: Combine the Cranberry Liqueur and Cocchi Rosa in a cocktail shaker with ice.

Stir, strain into a chilled champagne glass, and top off with champagne or crémant.

SERVING SUGGESTION: Float a cranberry or two on top as a garnish.

> Cocchi Rosa is an apéritif-style Italian wine that can be purchased online or at better liquor stores. It's worth seeking out as it has a much better taste in this cocktail than using another sweet vermouth.

— BRENNE CHAI TODDY —

Similar to the age-old hot toddy, your grandma's cure for a cold, this French version uses a very smooth French whisky aged in cognac barrels. But then we add Indian spiced Chai tea. You won't need a cold to drink this yummy concoction; any chilly day will create the right setting.

- **2 oz. Brenne Whisky (an incredibly smooth French-produced whisky)**
- **¼ cup of hot Chai tea**
- **½ tablespoon honey**
- **1 cinnamon stick**
- **1 star anise**

METHOD: Make tea and add honey and let steep. Add the whisky and spices. Sip and enjoy the warmth!

SERVING SUGGESTION: Serve with a cinnamon stick and slice of lemon.

This stunning creation by Jerome of Shake N' Smash uses products from Normandy, where Flaubert, the author of *L'Education Sentimentale,* was from.

- ½ oz. homemade chestnut honey syrup (see drink instructions below)
- 1¾ oz. Christian Drouin Calvados (or any other good Calvados)
- ½ oz. fresh lemon juice
- 1 tablespoon Domaine de Canton ginger liqueur or a crushed piece of ginger
- A pinch of cinnamon powder
- Hard cider

METHOD: First, make chestnut honey syrup using an equal amount of honey and hot water infused with chestnuts.

Take all the remaining ingredients except the cider and shake in a cocktail shaker with ice.

Strain and serve in a cognac glass on crushed ice, topping off with the cider. Add more crushed ice so it's nearly overflowing.

SERVING SUGGESTION: Garnish with several apple slices standing in the ice.

> At Shake n' Smash, this drink is served with a page from Flaubert's *L'Education Sentimentale* as a coaster.

This would make a very festive holiday season margarita, with a petite French touch.

- ½ oz. Pomegranate Liqueur (Edmond Briottet)
- 1 oz. Ocho Blanco tequila
- 1 tablespoon triple sec or Cointreau
- 2 teaspoons lime juice

METHOD: In a cocktail shaker, shake ingredients with ice, strain, and serve on the rocks in a chilled rocks glass with or without salt and a lime wedge.

SERVING SUGGESTION: Float several pomegranate seeds on top.

Bonne Fête!

HAPPY HOLIDAY!

(USED FOR A VARIETY OF HOLIDAYS)

— ARTISANAL COCKTAILS —

YUZU CORN 175

ZEITOUNI 179

CAPRIS C'EST FINI 184

ROSEBUD 185

BLOODY SECRET 187

FALUKA 188

DE LA BRETAGNE 190

EXPÉRIENCE 1 192

OLD CUBAN 193

BOBO PARISIEN 196

BLACK POINT À LA
FRANÇAISE 197

ROMEO À RIO 199

THE SMOKY SPICY
MARGARITA 200

IGGY 205

MOONFLOWER 207

MAZARINETTE 209

RED HOUSE OLD
FASHIONED 211

LIBERTINE 212

NIGHT BIRD 213

AUDEMUS CENTURY 214

FUEGO DE COLIMA 217

ESQUISSE NO.1 218

A CONQUISTADOR 221

LE PULPEUX 222

COFFEE OLD
FASHIONED 224

FAÇON MARIA 226

LE WOODY WOOD 227

Ready to get creative? The bars and their signature cocktails that I describe in this section are newsworthy ones, the scene setters, the artisanal (craft) bars that have set Paris on fire with excitement. Bartenders in Paris have come from Marseille, Minnesota, London, and beyond to create these unique recipes to thrill Parisians and expat palates alike. Many use homemade, French-made and small batch ingredients in a new, unique way. I paved a path from craft bar to artisan enclave to find the best of the best, presented below. While sometimes you'll need to search beyond your neighborhood liquor store for some ingredients, the fruits of your labors will be rewarded grandly.

> The popular craft bars listed here, particularly those that have tables, should be reserved ahead of time particularly on weekends to avoid an annoying waiting in line.

You've heard of craft beer but what the heck is a craft bar? How do you know you are in a craft bar as opposed to a regular pub or a fancy cocktail bar? It's all about the ingredients. Whether you are in Paris, New York, or London in a craft bar, you'll find more than ten types of bitters, a variety of fresh herbs, dried and fresh fruits—in other words, much more than your standard line up of lemon and lime wedges. At a craft bar, you'll also notice loads of different types of vermouths and bitter-flavored alcohols and you won't find what is traditionally called *well liquors*, those cheap brands that they automatically reach for when you order a standard drink.

Industrial brands such as Gordon's, Smirnoff, or Seagrams are strictly *verboten* at a craft bar because the word "craft" indicates a predilection for items that are homemade, made in small batches, or made in an artisanal fashion. There has been an effort worldwide on the part the millennial generation to get back to making things by hand, which has led to the rise of craft cocktails and craft bars. Don't be intimidated by the craft cocktail recipes in this chapter—if you can get your hands on the unique ingredients, they're worth making!

VALENTIN CALVEL,
BARTENDER AT APICIUS

• • •

"MY COCKTAIL, IT'S LIKE A PASSPORT FOR THEM, OR A FINGERPRINT—UNIQUE TO JUST THEM. THIS IS WHY I PREFER TO MAKE BESPOKE COCKTAILS AFTER TALKING TO MY GUEST. I LOVE GIVING HIM OR HER SOMETHING ONLY FOR THEM."

Valentin, the ingenious bartender at Apicius, has found a way to marry East (Yuzu Saki), West (New York Corn Whiskey), and Middle (Antique Sherry from Spain) in one delicious drink!

- Lemon cress
- 1¾ oz. Nigori Yuzushu
- 1⅓ oz. Hudson New York Corn Whiskey
- ½ oz. Sherry Fino antique from Fernando de Castillo
- 2 teaspoons Maraschino liqueur (Luxardo)
- 2 dashes honey
- Yuzu twist

METHOD: In a shaker, crush 6 lemon cress leaves with crushed ice.

Add Yuzushu, whiskey, Fino, Maraschino liqueur, and honey. Shake vigorously.

Double strain into an old-fashioned glass with a large ice ball.

SERVING SUGGESTION: Garnish with a yuzu lemon twist, a few leaves of lemon cress, and 2 Luxardo maraschino cherries. You can substitute a regular lemon if you can't obtain a yuzu.

An Artisianal Drinks Tasting Party

Invite your most adventurous friends for this very worldly craft cocktail and hors d'oeuvres pairing. Send out your invitations several weeks before this special cocktail party to allow yourself time to source all of the ingredients required, as well as the time to infuse the gin and make any other special ingredients required. Bon appetit!

Pick three of the more challenging recipes in this book, those that require you to make an ingredient ahead of time. Examples include the Alchimia Cocktail, Tijuana Swizzle, and Oh My Dog.

SERVE:

- **Alchimia Cocktail (page 37) brings Southeast Asian flair for vodka lovers**
- **The Tijuana Swizzle (page 44) brings in the warmth of Mexico for tequila lovers**
- **Oh My Dog (page 48) hints of a certain kind of proper Englishness**

NIBBLES:

- **Alongside each drink, serve an appropriate appetizer that will evoke the mood and flavor of each cocktail such as Vietnamese spring rolls with the Alchimia cocktail, guacamole and corn chips with the Swizzle, and smoked salmon canapés with Oh My Dog.**

- **For canapés simply spread some cream cheese (or
  fromage frais) onto a diagonally sliced English cucumber. Top with small slice of smoked salmon
  about the same size as the cucumber and garnish
  with a frond of dill. Make enough to serve several
  to each guest.**

Set out your serving plates of appetizers and give each person
one small appetizer plate so that they may sample each of the
items. Likewise give each person three *petit* glasses such as
sherry glasses. Allow them to try each cocktail with the accom-
panying appetizer pairing. If you choose the three cocktails
above, start with the gin and then move to vodka and finally tequila. Like wine, you'll want to taste from the lighter to the
more complex. And, of course, have fun!

ANDY WAHLOO

69 Rue Gravilliers, 75003 Paris
Phone: 01 42 71 20 38
Price: **
Atmosphere: Moroccan hipster
http://andywahloo-bar.com/

Kaled behind the bar is as passionate and knowledgeable about the art of cocktails as anyone you'll meet. His Zeitouni, made with vodka citron, lemongrass, olive oil, and pineapple is a refreshing long drink reminiscent of a warm night in Morocco. His Lorena Forever is a rum-based wonder named after the female distiller of the Zapata rum used in the cocktail. He'll surprise you with drinks made with dry ice and the smell of rosewater on the side for the fun of it, but these details are not just for show. His concoctions are enticing.

KALED DEROUCH
FROM ANDY WAHLOO

• • •

"IF YOU COME TO MY BAR TO DRINK BEER OR SPEND 1000 EUROS, I WANT YOU TO BE ABLE TO HAVE THE SAME EXPERIENCE—TO BE ABLE TO HAVE A GOOD COCKTAIL AND FORGET EVERYTHING AND JUST ENJOY."

From the creative mind of Kaled Derouch, chief bartender at Andy Wahloo. This drink is meant to evoke an afternoon in Morocco, the place from which Andy Wahloo and their neighboring resto, Derriere, draw their influence.

- 4 basil leaves
- 1 round of fresh pineapple
- Several slices of Granny Smith apple
- 2 teapoons of simple syrup
- 1 pinch of black pepper
- 1 pinch of salt
- 2 oz. Ketel One Citroën
- 1 teaspoon of olive oil

METHOD: Crush the basil leaves with crushed ice in a cocktail shaker and add the simple syrup. Add the pineapple and Granny Smith apple and mash until juiced.

Pour Ketel One and the olive oil into the mixture. Finish with a pinch of salt and pepper. Add ice and shake vigorously. Strain carefully and serve in a chilled coupe glass.

SERVING SUGGESTION: Garnish with a dried basil leaf (you may substitute fresh).

A la Française

50 rue Léon Frot 75011 Paris
Phone: 09 82 49 02 69
**Price: **
Atmosphere: 100% bar française

Head directly downstairs to the 70s-style drinking den. Chef du bar Stephen Miller is a historian of everything associated with French cocktail culture and products. He has virtually the only 100% French and Francophone bar stocked only with French products of which there is an amazing array. He serves up French cocktails that he's sourced back to the 1800s, and he is as passionate about the topic as anyone in the world. This is a cool craft bar, no doubt, but the interest here is for serious cocktail geeks and passionate Francophiles. This is *the* place to try some impossible-to-find French whiskies, vodkas, gins, and many more France products made in France. Santé!

Bespoke

3 Rue Oberkampf, 75011 Paris
Phone: 01 58 30 88 59
**Price: **
Atmosphere: Homey
http://bspk.fr/

Nicolas and Melissa and their teeny dog Bruce were among the most delightful bar owners I met in Paris. They opened their bar on the famed rue Oberkampf in 2014 when they were only 25. Marseille natives and together since the tender age of 15, this duo has created a very trendy place with snappy cocktails without any of the blow-off attitude often found in such places. Their Capri C'est Fini made with cherry tomatoes and rum (no, I'm not kidding) is absolutely astonishing.

NICOLAS CO-OWNER OF BESPOKE

• • •

"WE WANT PEOPLE TO FEEL FREE TO TRY SOMETHING THEY WOULDN'T NORMALLY TRY SO EVEN IF A DRINK IS PERFECTLY MADE YOU CAN SEND IT BACK IF YOU DON'T LIKE IT."

CAFÉ MODERNE

19 Rue Keller, 75011 Paris
Phone: 01 47 00 53 62
Price: **
Atmosphere: Late-night bistro
http://www.cafemoderne-tbmb.com/

Charming with an *oh-so-French* atmosphere complete with old French signs and a long wooden bar, these are the hallmarks of a classic French bar and bistro. Yet this place is modern in more than name only. They serve bang-up cocktails made by Mido, who was recently named the best bartender in France, and a menu of items that have been hashed, cut, or ground-up, such as meatballs, tartares, and burgers. Their burgers are damn good, as are their deliciously icy Londoner cocktail, similar to a mint julep but made with gin.

CANDELARIA

52 Rue de Saintonge, 75003 Paris
Phone: 01 42 74 41 28
Price: **
Atmosphere: Bubbling
http://www.candelariaparis.com/

You must be in the know to get in here; there is no sign, just a door at the back of a tiny little taco shack in the Marais. Once you walk through the door you'll be treated to scrumptious cocktails and a really vibrant scene. It's famous and it gets crowded so go early or late or on a weeknight and order a Saintonge Sprinz in summer or a Guêpe Verte in winter... *santé!*

Ça s'arrose!

THAT DESERVES A DRINK!

— CAPRI C'EST FINI —

Y ou will never believe this combo of fresh tomatoes and rum would taste this good. From the cunning minds behind the bar at Bespoke.

- 4 cherry tomatoes
- 2 basil leaves
- ½ oz. freshly squeeze lemon juice
- ½ oz. housemade sugarcane syrup (but you can use one that you bought in any local store)
- Half a bar spoon of balsamic vinegar
- ½ oz. Rum Plantation 3 stars

METHOD: Take a shaker, put in the tomatoes and basil leaves, muddle them, then add all the remaining ingredients, add ice cubes, and shake vigorously. Double strain in a chilled a coupe glass, g

SERVING SUGGESTION: Garnish with a mozzarella ball, basil leaf, and cherry tomato. Enjoy the awesomeness.

Ⓒ

A glittering cocktail created and served at Bespoke.

- ¼ oz. Hendrick's gin
- ½ tablespoon Reserva Carlos Alberto sweet vermouth
- ½ oz. Combier crème de rose
- ½ oz. housemade sugarcane syrup (but you can use one that you bought in any local store)
- ½ oz. freshly squeezed lemon juice
- 2 dashes cranberry bitters
- Fever Tree tonic water water (or other premium tonic)

METHOD: Take a shaker, pour in all the ingredients but the tonic water, shake vigorously, strain into a Collins glass full of ice cubes, and top with the tonic water.

SERVING SUGGESTION: Garnish with a rosebud.

Poisson, sans boisson—
c'est poison!

(TO EAT) FISH WITHOUT DRINKING
WINE IS POISON.

(THIS IS ALSO A TONGUE TWISTER.)

CASTOR CLUB

14 Rue Hautefeuille, 75006 Paris

Phone: 09 50 64 99 38

Price: **

Atmosphere: Upscale log cabin

I never thought I would want to spend time in a Tennessee cabin in Paris until I walked into this darling little bar in the 6th arrondissement. Try the John's Last Word with absinthe and celery juice for something unusual and terribly tasty.

COPPER BAY

5 Rue Bouchardon, 75010 Paris

Price: **

Atmosphere: Bright nautical

http://www.copperbay.fr/

This crisp, clean, bright nautically themed bar is owned by three friends, two of whom happen to be women. I'm always happy when I see women taking the helm behind the bar, and this experience was no different. Julien from Montpellier, Aurélie from Bretagne, and Elfi from Avignon greet you with extraordinary and atypical French kindness upon entry. Every season they select a group of classic cocktails to highlight such as sours or Collins or spritzes. They also will have six hand-crafted cocktails that highlight the season. I loved the Piss Pepe, served to me on a cold winter night. This was a hot toddy made with rum and honey laced with evergreens and served with a burning mini pinecone on top.

A tequila-oriented version of the Bloody Mary served with style by the ladies and gents at Copper Bay in Paris.

- 1⅓ oz. Tequila
- ¾ oz. fresh lemon juice
- ½ tablespoon of Magic Copper Bay potion, which consists of Worcestershire, Tabasco, jalapeno, BBQ spices, Cajun spices, horseradish, and smoked paprika according to your taste
- 6 dashes of roasted garlic bitters
- Serve with a small bottle of very high quality tomato juice (Granny's secret brand is preferred)

METHOD: Make this cocktail directly in the high-ball glass with 4 large cubes of ice, adding ingredients and stirring in the order they are shown. If you are able to find a very high-quality tomato juice in a small bottle, serve it on the side and let the recipient pour it in; if not, serve what you have in a small pitcher on the side to pour.

SERVING SUGGESTION: Garnish with 2 bay leaves, 1 pickled shallot, and 2 small dried red peppers.

— FALUKA —

A Faluka is a type of sailing boat used on the Nile. This drink created at Copper Bay will let you sail away to foreign lands.

- 1¾ oz. Pisco
- ⅓ oz. fresh lime juice
- ½ oz. Jellab (combination of date syrup, rose water, and roasted pine nuts)
- White of one egg

METHOD: Shake all ingredients, strain, and serve over ice in a rocks glass.

SERVING SUGGESTION: Garnish with pan masala.

Tu vas sortir ce soir?

ARE YOU GOING OUT TONIGHT?

— DE LA BRETAGNE —

Invented at the new Copper Bay bar, this cocktail that celebrates Brittany is supposed to be served at room temperature.

- 1 oz. rye whiskey
- ¾ oz. Pommeau de Bretagne
- ½ oz. Bénédictine liqueur
- ½ tablespoon hydromel like Tupelo Mead
- 4 dashes anise extract (found in the baker's section at your grocer)

METHOD: Pour all ingredients into a mixing glass without ice.

Aerate the liquid with a mini whisk and swizzle method.

SERVING SUGGESTION: Pour into tall hurricane glass rimmed with Cajun spices to create an emulsion.

Pommeau de Bretagne is a light alcoholic drink made with apple juice and Calvados (apple brandy). You can find it at quality liquor stores.

EXPERIMENTAL COCKTAIL CLUB (ECC)

37 Rue Saint-Sauveur, 75002 Paris
Phone: 01 45 08 88 09
Price: **
Atmosphere: Speakeasy
http://www.experimentalcocktailclub.fr/

This was the bar that changed everything in Paris and where the ECC group got its start. Now set to open their fourteenth place in just eight years, Experimental was where the magic began.

Going in now, it might not feel as groundbreaking as it was but back in 2007 when there were just hotel bars and bad bars (with a few exceptions). This groundbreaking lounge still looks and feels like a speakeasy: the small sign is hard to see, the ambiance is dark and sexy, and the drinks are heavenly. People took notice back then and a very cool crowd continues to make this intimate room their drinking hole.

ROMÉE DE GORIANINOFF,
ONE OF THE FOUNDERS
OF ECC

• • •

"ECC STARTED A NEW ICE CULTURE IN PARIS; WE BROUGHT IN THE FIRST AMERICAN-STYLE ICE MACHINES, WHICH ENABLED US TO OFFER A PROPER COCKTAIL USING ALL DIFFERENT TYPES OF ICE."

One of the first cocktails created by Romée and his partners when they opened Experimental Cocktail Club. It's one of the first and only to survive the later cocktail lists at their various clubs around the world.

- 1¾ oz. vodka
- ½ teaspoon fresh lemon juice
- ½ teaspoon elderflower cordial
- 2 fresh basil leaves

METHOD: Shake the ingredients together with ice in your cocktail shaker. Strain twice and serve in a chilled martini glass.

SERVING SUGGESTION: ECC garnishes this drink with a lemon grass straw.

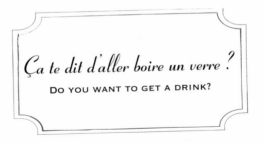

Ça te dit d'aller boire un verre ?

DO YOU WANT TO GET A DRINK?

This is ECC's take on the cocktail originally created by Audrey Saunders of the Pegu Club.

- Fresh mint leaves
- ½ oz. lime juice
- 1 ⅓ oz. Ron Cubain Havana club 3 years (or your favorite premium white rum)
- ½ oz. simple syrup
- 1 barspoon of ginger cordial
- Billecart Salmon brut champagne to top
- 2 dashes of Angostura bitters on top

METHOD: Shake all ingredients except the champagne and bitters.

SERVING SUGGESTION: Serve in a chilled martini glass without ice. Top off with the champagne and bitters.

Jefrey's

14 Rue Saint-Sauveur, 75002 Paris
Phone: 01 42 33 60 77
Price: **
Atmosphere: Intimate lounge
http://www.jefreys.fr/

After or before a visit to the ECC stop into Jefrey's just across the street. This tiny little place modeled after an English gentleman's club is definitely not for guys only. With Guillaume Bizio behind the bar, this is the place to try something new and interesting. Guillaume did time at three different Palace hotels; he makes his own bitters (more than 15 types) and is offering cutting-edge cocktails in every sense of the word. I loved the Bobo Parisian, a concoction not too sweet, not too strong, and served in a teacup.

Glass

7 Rue Frochot, 75009 Paris, France
Phone: 09 80 72 98 83
Price: **
Atmosphere: Intimate
http://www.glassparis.com/

In the now über-trendy So-Pi neighborhood is yet another late-night hotspot brought to you by the folks behind Candelaria. Try the John Doe, which contains Pisco flavored with dill, Fenet Branca, and their house-made lime cordial. It's light green, fresh, and delectable.

— BOBO PARISIEN —

This delightful cocktail comes from the ingenious brain of Guillaume at Jefrey's bar in the 2nd arrondissement, Paris.

- 1¾ oz. gin (Tanqueray preferred)
- ½ oz. St. Germain
- ½ oz. King L'Avion d'Or
- 1 dash of rhubarb bitters
- The whites of one egg
- And a splash of club soda

METHOD: Shake all ingredients together with ice in a cocktail shaker.

SERVING SUGGESTION: Serve in an oversized tea cup with a whole star anise floating in the froth and a sprinkling of Peychaud bitters. Watch your friends smile.

This is a strong drink for a whisky lover devised by Guillaume, the *chef du bar* at Jefrey's. It's important to serve it in a small, chilled sherry or port glass.

- 1½ oz. JW Double Black Whisky
- ½ tablespoon Picon Club
- ½ tablespoon Yellow Chartreuse
- 1 teaspoon Grand Marnier

METHOD: Mix all ingredients together and serve in an elegant Nick and Nora–style glass (sherry or port) and garnish with a dried orange round.

Je prends, (un verre de rosé), s'il vous plaît.

(FILL IN THE COCKTAIL NAME)
I'LL TAKE (A GLASS OF ROSE) PLEASE.

La Conserverie

37 Rue du Sentier, 75002 Paris
Phone: 01 40 26 14 94
Price: **
Atmosphere: Boudoir-chic
www.laconserveriebar.com
http://www.uc-61.com/

Named after those little jars used to conserve our homemade jam, this hotspot opened just a year or so after Experimental Cocktail Club (ECC) and follows the sexy, boudoir, speakeasy trend that has seen such success in Paris. The decor is inventive, warm, and tasteful, lights are low, and Romain Krot at the bar exudes charm. We enjoyed the cocktail of the month, the Piste Vert (the green or bunny slope) with Sapin liqueur, made from evergreen trees, along with the rabbit pâté.

Le Calbar

82 Rue de Charenton, 75012 Paris
Phone: 01 84 06 18 90
Price: **
Atmosphere: A single girl's dream
http://lecalbarcocktail.com/

Pretty quickly upon entering this bar you'll realize that the name means "boxer shorts" in French slang because that's all the guys are wearing apart from their shirts. If you can take your eyes off of their legs, you'll enjoy the cool decor, black walls and all kinds of small paintings, small copper pots, and other bric-a-brac adorning *les murs*. Oh yeah, and the drinks are pretty darn good, too.

Christophe Sichanh, bartender and co-founder at Calbar

•••

"Here our most popular drink is the 'Surprise Me,' which is when our bartenders make a bespoke cocktail just for you and the mood you are in."

— ROMEO À RIO —

A Brazilian Romeo is certainly fantasy worthy. Perhaps this will get you halfway there. By Romain at La Conserverie.

- ½ oz. red fruit syrup
- ½ oz. fresh lemon juice
- 1¾ oz. Cachaça (a Brazilian-made sugar cane liquor)
- 1 barspoon of Liqueur de Violette
- A few mint sprigs
- 1 egg white

METHOD: Make red fruit syrup by infusing simple syrup with raspberries and strawberries. Cool and strain before use.

Shake ingredients dry (that is, without ice) and then wet (with ice), and strain into a chilled martini glass.

SERVING SUGGESTION: At La Conserverie, this drink is sprinkled with smoked paprika.

> Liqueur de Violette (also Crème de Violette) is actually made with real violets by a number of different companies in France and elsewhere such as Briottet and Giffard. It is widely available online and at high-end liquor stores.

— THE SMOKY SPICY MARGARITA —

The guys in their underwear at Calbar in Paris concocted this number, and yes, it's delish!

- 1⅓ oz. Mezcal vida
- ½ tablespoon Islay whisky
- 1 oz. fresh lime juice

- ³/₅ oz. homemade red pepper syrup (create this by adding spicy red peppers to your simple syrup and let stand as long as possible)
- ½ tablespoon Campari
- 3 dashes of Thai bitters

METHOD: Shake all ingredients with ice, double strain, and serve in a chilled martini glass and garnish with a dried orange wheel. Feel free to drink in your boxer shorts!

Je voudrais votre meilleur cocktail.

I'D LIKE TO HAVE YOUR BEST COCKTAIL.

Le Mary Celeste

1 Rue Commines, 75003 Paris
Phone: 09 80 72 98 83
Price: **
Atmosphere: Nautical
http://www.lemaryceleste.com/

A refreshingly unique little bar decorated in white with a few pops of color. The sphere shaped bar is inviting, as is the variety of small bites on offer including oysters, which most other bars don't offer.

L'Entrée des Artistes

30-32 rue Victor Massé - 75009 Paris
Phone: 01 45 23 11 93
Price: **
Atmosphere: Jazzy speakeasy
http://www.lentreedesartistespigalle.com/

This chic little place is one of my favorite bars—the interior looks like a cross between a joint you'd find in Argentina mixed with enough French-ness to make it feel at home in Paris. There is no sign outside, just the address, a little smoking station, and a bar license sign to indicate that you should go inside for mind-bogglingly good drinks. I loved both the Bon and the Chicha-rito (a spicy take on a margarita but with cucumber). DJs take over on weekends, making this near-perfect bar difficult to leave. Reserve in advance.

Le Syndicat

51 rue Faubourg St Denis, 75010 Paris
Phone: 06 66 63 57 60
Price: **
Atmosphere: Urban grunge
http://www.syndicatcocktailclub.com/

Le Syndicat is a fun and friendly place that has an adorably sexy *chef du bar*. Sullivan creates outrageous concoctions made with burning orange bark (the Smoking Car) or Pastis (the Sudiste). He specializes in using French-made ingredients, and the results are superb. The hip-hop in the background creates a *trés cool* ambiance.

Mabel

58 rue d'Aboukir, 75002 Paris
Phone: 06 66 63 57 60
Price: **
Atmosphere: The classic cocktail bar
http://www.mabelparis.com/

This self-proclaimed Rum Empire is the place to hit if you're a real rum fan. Creator Joseph Akhavan, like Michael at Maria Loca and the folks at Dirty Dick, just loves rum. On offer are over 100 rums and a cocktail list that graciously veers away from the punchy/fruity numbers that most people feel you must serve with the sugar cane liquor. I tried the Sombre Detune, which was strong, smoky, and smooth, with no fruit at all. For me, this was a welcome relief.

Little Red Door

60 rue Charlot, 75003 Paris
Phone: 09 83 58 93 32
Price: **
Atmosphere: Cocktail tavern
http://www.lrdparis.com/

Don't attempt to actually enter the little red door like I did; instead open the actual door on the left and you won't feel so foolish. Have a seat at the bar and order up a Poor Willy's Mule or an Iggy. They are sincere about their craft at Little Red Door; interestingly, they add a douse of homemade saltwater to each recipe, which they feel brings all the ingredients together. And why not; chefs have been doing this forever in the kitchen. Located on the rue Charlot, one of the coolest streets in Paris, this hotspot sizzles with class and cocktail expertise.

This pop-star cocktail was invented at the Little Red Door in Paris.

- • 1½ oz. Dolin Dry Vermouth
- • ¾ oz. Merlet Brothers blend cognac
- • 1 tablespoon Eucalyptus syrup
- • 4 dashes Braulio Italian bitter liqueur (or any Italian Amaro)
- • Dash of salt solution

METHOD: All of the ingredients are stirred over ice and then strained and served in a chilled martini glass.

SERVING SUGGESTION: Garnish with grapefruit zest.

WILLIAM AT LITTLE RED DOOR

• • •

"AT THE LITTLE RED DOOR WE USE A SALT SOLUTION IN ALL OF OUR DRINKS, AND THEY ALSO DO THAT AT LULU WHITE. I'M NOT SURE IF ANYONE ELSE IS DOING IT, BUT WE FEEL THAT IT MARRIES THE INGREDIENTS TOGETHER AND EMPHASIZES FLAVOR JUST LIKE SALT DOES FOR FOOD. WE'VE DONE TASTE TESTS, AND A DRINK MADE WITH THE SOLUTION IS MUCH BETTER THAN WITHOUT."

LULU WHITE

12 Rue Frochot, 75009 Paris
Phone: 09 83 58 93 32
Price: **
Atmosphere: Paris meets New Orleans
http://www.luluwhite.bar/

This absinthe bar named in honor of a renowned New Orleans Madame attempts to combine the spirit of Pigalle where it's located with sense of *Nouvelle Orleans*. The result is a charming and warm mélange with two Brits mixing drinks behind the bar. Even if you don't speak French you can learn a lot here about the new Paris cocktail culture by talking to Matthew Long, the head bartender. Absinthe is revered at Lulu White but fear not, they are expert at putting just a hint of it in their craftily made drinks.

— MOONFLOWER —

c

nvented by Matthew Long, head bartender at Lulu White, this is a push-me pull-you type of drink. Come down with the scotch and stay up with the coffee. Perfect when you need that pick-me-up at 11 p.m.

- 1½ oz. Chivas 12 Year Scotch
- 2 oz. Cold Brew Coffee (weaker coffee is best)
- ½ oz. Dubonnet Rouge
- 5 drops St. George Vert Absinthe
- 1 tablespoon Perrier

METHOD: Combine ingredients, except Perrier, in a mixing glass.

Gently stir for 3 seconds, strain into ice filled Collins glass, and add Perrier. Mix thoroughly.

SERVING SUGGESTION: Garnish with a lemon slice and a straw.

"LET ME BE MAD, THEN, BY ALL MEANS! MAD WITH THE MADNESS OF ABSINTHE, THE WILDEST, MOST LUXURIOUS MADNESS IN THE WORLD! VIVE LA FOLIE! VIVE L'AMOUR! VIVE L'ANIMALISME! VIVE LE DIABLE!"

Marie Corelli, Wormwood: A Drama of Paris

PARIS COCKTAILS —207

Pas de Loup

108 Rue Amelot, 75011 Paris
Phone: 09 54 74 16 36
Price: **
Atmosphere: Inventively beautiful
http://www.pasdeloupparis.com/

At this lovely bar and resto right next to the Cirque Hiver I experienced all kinds of surprising taste sensations. Try the Bloody Celeri for a completely out-of-the box take on a Bloody Mary, sans tomato juice. Yes, you heard right, but it gets a deliciously fresh tomato flavor from the dehydrated tomato which rims the glass. Inventive and incredibly delicious.

Prescription Cocktail Club

23 rue Mazarine, 75006 Paris
Phone: 09 50 35 72 87
Price: **
Atmosphere: Rendez-vous
http://www.prescriptioncocktailclub.com/

This is the ECC outlet in St. Germain, with a larger space but the same successful formula: good service, superior bar craft, and dark and sexy ambiance. Order the Mazarinette, named in honor of the street that Prescription sits on, if you want something fruity and easy to drink.

— MAZARINETTE —

©

This is the signature cocktail made at the Prescription Cocktail Club in the 6th, St. Germain, Paris.

- 1 tablespoon lemon juice
- 1 tablespoon homemade rhubarb juice
- 1 oz. Gordon sloe gin liqueur (or your favorite sloe gin)
- ¾ oz. gin
- 1 oz. Sipsmith Summer Cup apéritif
- Champagne to top

METHOD: Make your own rhubarb juice using frozen or fresh rhubarb, one bunch chopped into ¾-inch pieces. Cover with water and simmer for about 30 minutes. Strain through a mesh, cool, and your juice is ready to use. Can be stored in your refrigerator for up to a week.

Shake all items except champagne with ice, strain into chilled martini glass, and serve neat, topped with champagne.

SERVING SUGGESTION: Garnish with a strawberry.

Sipsmith is a fairly new small batch liquor company headquartered in the UK and partly owned by Jared Brown, one of the world's most well-known cocktail historians; coincidentally, I consulted him for this book. Their Summer Cup is a gin infused with the flavors of Earl Grey tea and lemon verbena grown by Jared himself, a very English gin indeed.

What's the difference between gin and sloe gin? Gin is a liquor traditionally made with juniper berries. Sloe gin is actually a liqueur, not a liquor, made with berries from the blackthorn bush and is red in color and sweet in taste.

RED HOUSE

1 bis Rue de la Forge Royale, 75011
Paris, France
Phone: 01 43 67 06 43
Price: **
Atmosphere: Manly grunge

Late nights, a little grunge, an old school arcade game, real rock and roll on the radio—this is the kind of combo I can really get into. Red House feels very Brooklyn, yet you are right in the 11th arrondissement, the *vrai* night life area of Paris. This is the perfect place to end up after a long night. Their Red House Old Fashioneds are delicious, and yeah, it's okay to get a little sloppy here.

— RED HOUSE OLD FASHIONED —

Nobody makes an Old Fashioned like the Red House. Delicious!

- 1 cardamom seed
- 1 oz. Jim Beam Rye
- ½ oz. Bitter Truth Pimento Dram
- ½ oz. Drambuie

METHOD: Crush the cardamom in a mixing glass.

Add the remaining ingredients and stir with ice.

SERVING SUGGESTION: Serve on an ice ball (or large cube) in a double old-fashioned glass, garnished with a lemon peel and orange.

Tout arrive en France!

EVERYTHING HAPPENS IN FRANCE!
(FROM MAXIMES, RÉFLEXIONS MORALES BY
FRANÇOIS DE LA ROCHEFOUCAULD)

— LIBERTINE —

A libertine is described as a free-thinker, a man who disregards the social norms, especially in regards to sexuality. Whoa, look out ladies! This comes courtesy of Jen Riley from Red House, Paris.

- 1 oz. vodka
- 2 teaspoons campari
- 2 teaspoons simple syrup
- 2 teaspoons lemon juice
- 1 tablespoon grapefruit juice
- ½ oz. egg white
- 1 barspoon of rhubarb and ginger jam

METHOD: Shake all ingredients together with ice in a shaker.

Double strain and shake again without ice to emulsify the egg white, then pour into a champagne flute and top with ½ oz. Ruby Port.

JEN RILEY,

BARTENDER AT RED HOUSE

• • •

"IN PARIS, IT WAS DIFFICULT FOR WOMEN AT BARS WHEN I FIRST STARTED. SOME PEOPLE WOULD HARDLY ORDER A DRINK FROM YOU BECAUSE THEY FELT LIKE YOU WOULDN'T KNOW WHAT YOU WERE DOING. FINALLY NOW I FEEL PARIS IS ON THE CUSP OF CHANGING WITH SO MANY MORE WOMEN BEHIND THE BAR; MEN ARE REALIZING WHAT A GREAT JOB WE'RE DOING."

A craft scotch cocktail by Jen Riley at Red House, Paris.

- 1¾ oz. Talisker Storm
- 1 barspoon Calvados gum syrup
- 5 dashes Creme de Violette
- 2 drops Teapot Bitters (available online from Boker's Bitters)

METHOD: Stirred over ice in a mixing glass and served into a chilled martini glass.

SERVING SUGGESTION: Garnish with a spray of bergamot essence.

> Bourbon isn't easily found in France, but if you prefer something a bit sweet, substitute bourbon in one of our whiskey recipes.

— AUDEMUS CENTURY —

Created by Joseph Boley at Red House, Paris, one of the most rock and roll bars in Paris. Great for a late-night tipple.

- 1 oz. Pink Pepper Gin (made by Audemus)
- ¾ oz. Cocchi Americano (similar to Dubonnet)
- ¾ oz. Crème de Cacao Blanc (white chocolate liqueur)
- ¾ oz. lemon juice

METHOD: Shake with ice in your shaker, strain, and pour into a chilled coupe glass neat.

SERVING SUGGESTION: Garnish with a lemon twist.

At this time Audemus is only available in Europe and the UK. Until it is distributed in the U.S. and Canada you can make your own by adding ½ tablespoon of pink peppercorns to a bottle of gin and let it sit for at least a day but as long as possible. Audemus doesn't crack their peppercorns, but other DIY-ers do.

Shake N' Smash

87, rue de Turbigo, 75003 Paris
Phone: 01 42 72 30 76
Price: **
Atmosphere: Funky finesse
http://shakensmash.com/

Jerome, the owner, is the fourth generation in business in the spot where his Corsican grandfather started a brasserie in 1923. Jerome recently changed the concept and created a true cocktail bar with a boudoir-style ambiance. Upon entry you might think you've entered a house of ill repute, but fear not; the only thing for sale is dangerously delicious cocktails and French-style tapas. I was wowed by the presentation and the taste of l'Education Sentimentale. It's inspired by the Flaubert novel and served on a page of the book in a cognac glass laying on its side on crushed ice with caramelized apples sticking out of the ice. The interior decor maybe funky, but Jerome is dead serious about his creative concoctions.

This inventive cocktail that combines ginger and lemongrass to tickle your taste buds is by Jerome at Shake N' Smash.

- 1¾ oz. Calle 23 tequila (any other good tequila)
- ¾ oz. ginger and lemongrass cordial (see recipe below)
- 2 teaspoons Chairman's Reserve Spiced Rum
- 1 tablespoon sugar syrup

FIRST, THE GINGER AND LEMONGRASS CORDIAL: A ginger and lemongrass non-alcoholic cordial is made by Bottlegreen in Britain but tough to source in the States. So here's how you can make your own. You'll need: a large nob of ginger peeled and sliced, and a stick of lemongrass (crush the white part and chop finely discarding any green parts). Add ginger and lemongrass to 2 cups water and 1½ cups sugar. Let sugar dissolve over the heat on simmer as you would any simple syrup. Let the flavors simmer together for about 20 minutes. Cool, strain, and add to a jar storing it in the fridge up to two weeks or more.

METHOD: Mix all ingredients together and shake with ice.

SERVING SUGGESTION: Served in a chilled coupe glass.

An esquisse is a preliminary sketch. This sketch was created by Jerome at Shake N' Smash, Paris.

- 1¾ oz. Grey Goose Pear (or other pear vodka)
- 1½ oz. white chardonnay grape juice by Alain Millat (or other fine-quality white grape juice)
- 4 teaspoons fresh squeezed grapefruit
- 4 teaspoons fresh squeezed lime
- 1½ tablespoon homemade vanilla syrup (or substitute other vanilla syrup, like Monin, for example)

METHOD: Place all ingredients in a cocktail shaker with ice and shake vigorously.

Strain and serve in a coupe glass.

SERVING SUGGESTION: Hang several grapes over the edge of the glass, as well as a slice of fresh pear that's been soaked in lemon juice and water so that it doesn't brown.

JEROME, OWNER OF SHAKE N' SMASH

• • •

"IT'S ALL ABOUT THE ART AND PASSION OF THE CREATION AND THE INGREDIENTS."

UNIQUE

This group of bars in Paris were founded on a theme or an area of interest that the owners are passionate about. These will be difficult to find elsewhere, and if they spur your imagination as they did mine, go ahead and belly up to the bar.

BATON ROUGE

62 Rue Notre Dame de Lorette, 75009 Paris
Phone: 06 98 51 57 22
Price: *
Atmosphere: New Orleans voodoo

One of my all-around favorite bars. Joseph Biolatto, the co-founder and bartender, is uncharacteristically tall and strapping for a Frenchman and disarmingly welcoming. Inspired by Louisiana, voodoo, and American nonchalance, Baton Rouge is at once a chic bar with extremely unique and tasty cocktails and a place where you can throw your peanut shells on the floor. If it were closer to me, I'd make this my local. Don't miss the voodoo corner lit up by candles, *j'adore ça.*

COMPTOIR GENERALE

80 quai de Jemmapes, Paris 75010
Phone: 01 44 88 24 48
Price: *
Atmosphere: Eclectic & blooming
http://www.lecomptoirgeneral.com/

Places like this in Paris are priceless. Creativity rules here; it's a gallery, it's a museum, a bookshop, a café, and yeah, there are cocktails. Their signature cocktail is Secousse with bissap, a Senegalese liqueur made from hibiscus flowers. I love the high ceilings, the quirky flea market décor, and the general vibe. They call it a museum of ghetto culture; I call it wonderful.

Gossima Ping Pong Bar

4 Rue Victor Gelez, 75011 Paris
Phone: 09 67 29 75 79
Price: **
Atmosphere: Competitive fun
http://www.gossima.fr/

The Gossima Ping Pong bar is the place to go with a bunch of friends. It's ideal for students and anyone who enjoys ping pong, but it's also hip and serves up a mean cocktail. Talk to Thomas at the bar; he'll invent something for you. Or, sample his Conquistador, which is kind of like a margarita but made with a touch of chocolate, cacao, and spice.

Created by Nicolas and the boys at the super fun Ping Pong bar.

- ½ oz. Téquila Olmeca Reposado
- ½ oz. Téquila Olmeca Silver
- 1 tablespoon de liqueur de cacao blanc by Giffard
- ½ oz. fresh lime juice
- 1 teaspoon agave syrup
- 5–7 dashes Aztec chocolate bitters by Fee Bros.

METHOD: Combine all ingredients in a cocktail shaker with ice, shake, and strain.

SERVING SUGGESTION: Serve in a rocks glass with spicy salt on the rim and a lime wedge.

Il est très mignon, le barman!

THE BARTENDER IS REALLY CUTE!

Created by Nicolas Servettaz at the Gossima Ping Pong Bar, this is a refreshing cocktail for summer.

- 1½ oz. Beefeater Gin
- ½ oz. thyme liqueur (Bigallet brand)
- ½ oz. grapefruit juice
- ½ oz. fresh lime juice

METHOD: Mix all ingredients in a cocktail shaker with ice, strain, and serve over ice in a highball glass with ice and top with ginger beer.

SERVING SUGGESTION: Serve with a cucumber round and perhaps a fresh thyme sprig.

Que la fête commence!

LET THE PARTY BEGIN!

Wall St. Bar

17 Avenue Parmentier, 75011 Paris
Phone: 06 62 12 15 91
Price: *
Atmosphere: New York Stock
Exchange
http://wallstreetbar.fr/

If you ever dreamed of drinking at the Stock Exchange, you've come to the right place. What is lacking in ambiance is made up by the inventive concept of paying for your drinks depending on the fluctuations of the ticker. Your martini may go up or down as the clock ticks on, and it pays to order quickly when you see the price drop. Several times a night there's a stock market crash and drinks go down to their base levels; then you must shout out your order in the hundred seconds that remain.

Death by Burrito

4 Rue de la Fontaine au Roi, 75011
Paris
Phone: 01 43 55 14 40
Price: **
Atmosphere: Mexican cocktail bar
http://www.deathbyburrito.com/

A hipster hotspot offering only cocktails made with agave-based liquors. Yes, they have shots, but in order to appreciate it fully, try one of their finer sipping tequilas or mezcals. The guac is great and the fish tacos are petite, fresh, and tasty, but no, they don't have burritos—what?!

— COFFEE OLD FASHIONED —

This delicious drink was created by Candace Knyf as Death by Burrito's special during Paris' first-ever cocktail week in January 2015.

- **2 oz. tequila reposado infused with coffee**
- **1 barspoon agave syrup**
- **3 dashes Angostura bitters**

METHOD: First, infuse the tequila reposado with coffee. Put 3 barspoons of coffee in a filter submerged in 6 oz. of the tequila and let sit 4 hours to soak in the flavor.

Light a stick of cinnamon until it smolders on one end. Place on a plate and cover it with a rocks glass so the smoke accumulates in the glass.

Combine the remaining ingredients in a mixing glass.

Upend the rock glass and strain the drink into it adding a few cubes of ice.

THE CHAMBER

http://www.thechamberparis.com/
Price: **
Atmosphere: Exclusive yet friendly

This private, members-only cocktail club was started by my friend Forest Collins of @52Martini fame. Forest, who has written for my website Girls' Guide to Paris, is one of the foremost experts on the bar scene in Paris. If you join as a yearly member, she'll invite you to her exclusive and alluring events each week such as a pop-up absinthe bar. If you are visiting, you can drop in and pay a fee of 20 euros or so if you email her in advance. If you are into cocktails, this pop-up adventure in a secret apartment in Paris is one of the coolest things you can do.

MARIA LOCA

31 Boulevard Henri IV, 75004 Paris
Phone: 01 42 77 51 95
Price: **
Atmosphere: Shipwrecked
http://www.marialoca.com/

Head to Maria Loca if you like rum or cachaça; owner Michael and his partner are dead serious about the stuff. They take high-

quality rum and add their own mix of spices to them or macerate walnuts in cachaça, adding to and playing with the liquors and then creating wholly unique cocktails with their new products. Try the Façon Maria or Le Woody Wood and you'll walk away for a whole new appreciation for these liquors. Close your eyes, listen to the reggae, take a sip or two, and you'll feel like you are at a beach bar in St. Bart's.

reated by the charming Michael Landart at Maria Loca bar on Blvd Henri IV in Paris.

- 1¾ oz. Maria Loca Spiced Rum (or Chairman's Reserve Spiced Rum)
- 3 dashes Angostura bitters
- 1 barspoon Virgin Cane Honey

METHOD: Stir rum, bitters, and honey together in a cocktail glass with ice, and strain.

SERVING SUGGESTION: Serve over ice in an old-fashioned glass, no garnish.

MICHAEL LANDARF,

CO-OWNER OF MARIA LOCA

• • •

"MARIA LOCA IS NAMED AFTER THE ILLEGAL ALCOHOL THAT THEY MAKE IN PRISON FROM WHATEVER SCRAPS THEY CAN GET. WHERE THERE'S A WILL..."

A creative cocktail by a creative man, Michael Landart, co-founder of Maria Loca.

- **1⅓ oz. Cachaça infused with walnuts (the liquor only needs 30–60 minutes to infuse)**
- **½ oz. Calvados**
- **1 tablespoon Bénédictine**
- **1 tablespoon Orange Curacao**

METHOD: Serve ingredients on ice in a large wine glass and strain.

SERVING SUGGESTION: Hang half a walnut over the edge of the glass, and serve with a cinnamon stick swizzle.

Faire un tabac

BEING THE TOAST OF THE TOWN

LONDON

AMUSE BOUCHE

51 Parsons Green Lane London SW6
4JA, United Kingdom
+44 20 7371 8517
Price: **
Atmosphere: Sparkling farmhouse
http://www.amusebouchelondon.com/

Nibble on hand-crafted English cheese while sipping bubbly from France in a simple farmhouse-like setting. This champagne bar with cocktails shares space with Claude's kitchen that serves up some seriously good food done with rustic, creative flair using locally sourced English ingredients.

EXPERIMENTAL COCKTAIL CLUB

13 a Gerrard St., Chinatown, London
W1D 5PS
+44 20 7434 3559
Price: **
Atmosphere: Chinatown speakeasy
http://www.chinatownecc.com/

Naturally, London is important enough to score its own ECC brought to you by the boys from Paris. This version stays with the speakeasy theme, so you'll have to hunt it down in London's Chinatown. Once inside you'll find the same boudoir charm and strong, spirited cocktails.

MONTREAL

LE LAB

1351 Rachel East Montreal H2J 2K2, Canada
(514) 544-1333
Price: **
Atmosphere: Mad scientist
http://barlelab.com/

Let's face it—everything has a French spin in Montreal; it's the French-est city we've got in North America even though most of its residents also speak perfect English. Enter Le Lab, where cocktail culture is turned upside down. Cocktails with beef jerky in them, cocktails on fire, bartenders who juggle—no, this is not a literal circus bar; it's a cocktail lab where almost anything goes.

La Société (LS)

131 Bloor St. W. #211 Toronto, ON
M5S 1R1, Canada
(416) 551-9929
Price: **
Atmosphere: Classic tavern
http://toronto.lasociete.ca/

With a long zinc bar and a stained glass ceiling that is reminiscent of La Coupole or Bofinger in Paris, La Société will make any Francophile feel at home. Sit at the bar, share a petit seafood tower, and savor your French cocktails, such as Confort Parisien or the French Derby. You won't feel far from France.

Vancouver

Tableau Bar & Bistro

1181 Melville St. Vancouver, BC V6E
0A3, Canada
(604) 639-8692
Price: **
Atmosphere: Posh bistro
http://tableaubarbistro.com/

Try a De la Louisianne cocktail made with rye, sweet vermouth, Bénédictine, bitters, and absinthe, or a Delmonico mixed with Hennessy, sweet and dry vermouth, gin, and bitters. Share some moules frites with a friend in Tableau's beautifully stylish room.

"London is a riddle. Paris is an explanation."

G.K. Chesterton

— FRANCOPHILE IN THE USA —

WHISKY SOUR CERISE 234

MARDI GRAS WINE COCKTAILS 237

SAZERAC 238

VIEUX CARRÉ 239

PINK PANTHER 243

JOY DIVISION 245

SADE'S TABOO 246

BARON OF BROOKLYN 247

MAISON ABSINTHE COLADA 249

THE LAST WORD 259

Americans' love of France goes back hundreds of years and, contrary to what you've heard, the French are quite keen on the U.S. as well. There is nary a Parisian who won't tell you how much they love New York City, California, and Miami. There are certain towns in the U.S. that have an ingrained French-ness to their culture, namely New Orleans. Considering that there are now two bars in Paris dedicated to Louisiana-style cocktails and décor, the French revere this great town, too. Who doesn't love a place that invented jazz and the Sazerac? There are loads of French people living in San Francisco, New York, and Miami and they need places to drink. Thanks to the Alliance Française and a number of other French organizations, there is an interest in France all over the States. With that Francophile passion, you'll find bars and bistros serving up *un petite* slice of Paris daily.

A French-ified version of a true American classic.

- 1½ oz. Brenne Whisky (or another sweet whisky such as Jameson's)
- 1–2 oz. fresh lemon juice
- 1½ teaspoons simple syrup
- 1½ teaspoons Luxardo maraschino liqueur
- Cherries for garnish

METHOD: Add all ingredients in a cocktail shaker with ice.

Shake, strain and serve over ice in a rocks glass.

SERVING SUGGESTION: Garnish with Luxardo maraschino cherries or other cocktail cherries.

Mardi Gras Fête

Mardi is *Tuesday* in French. The tradition began with people eating all the leftover fatty foods (*fat* in French is *gras*) before the season of lent began when Christians usually gave up something like sweets, meat, or alcohol. A proper Mardi Gras parade occurs in Marseille, but most of France celebrates Pancake Day instead of Mardi Gras or Carnival. I say, combine the two and host a party on Fat Tuesday or February 2, when in France we are celebrating "'Fête de la Chandeleur'" also called "'Fête de la Lumière,'" or "'jour des crêpes.'"

DRINKS:
Sazerac (page 119) • Vieux Carré (page 239) • Mardi Gras Wine Cocktails (page 237)

NIBBLES:
Galette du Roi, **or King Cake, can be bought or made.**
Traditionally, crêpes are served. Serve a variety including:
Ham, cheese, and mushrooms
Lemon, sugar, and Nutella

   Buy Mardi Gras beads and masks to hand out to guests as they arrive. Dressing up in Mardi Gras colors is encouraged (purple and green). New Orleans and Dixieland jazz should be playing.Guests can do tricks, recite a poem, or tell a joke to get a set of beads from the bead master (or host). The one with the most beads at the end of the night wins a silly Mardi Gras–themed prize.

MARDI GRAS WINE COCKTAILS

Mardi Gras colors are purple, yellow and green. Add a drop of crème de violette to a glass of white wine to make it turn light purple, do the same with crème de menthe and some affordable sparkling wine. Line up a row of the purple white wines, a row of green champagne, and another row of plain white wine and, voilà, you've got your all of your colors and a celebration! If you want to get really fancy, float an edible violet on top of the glass. For the wine, use a Loire or Bordeaux white wine—nothing expensive.

C reated at the Roosevelt Hotel in New Orleans, this is a classic American cocktail with French origins.

- ½ teaspoon absinthe, or Herbsaint (a New Orleans brand of anise liqueur)
- 1 teaspoon simple syrup
- 4 dashes Peychaud bitters
- 1 small dash Angostura bitters
- 2 ounces rye whiskey
- Strip of lemon peel

METHOD: Fill a rocks glass with ice that has been coated with absinthe or Herbsaint.

Blend the whiskey and bitters with the simple syrup in a cocktail glass with ice and stir.

Strain this mixture into your rocks glass with the ice.

SERVING SUGGESTION: Rub lemon peel on the rim and serve with the peel on the rim and not in the drink.

> Originally a Sazerac was made with cognac, absinthe, a sugar cube, and three dashes of Pechaud's bitters, which was made in New Orleans by a local apothecary. Later Rye was substituted for the Cognac when French vineyards fell to the Phylloxera epidemic in the 1860s. Herbsaint replaced absinthe when it was banned in the U.S. in 1912. The Sazerac remains by law New Orleans' official cocktail.

— VIEUX CARRÉ —

Created in New Orleans in the 1930s this is as classic a Nawlins' cocktail as you can get. It is French for the *Old Square,* which refers to the French quarter.

- ¾ oz. rye whiskey
- ¾ oz. cognac
- ¾ oz. sweet vermouth
- A dash of both Peychaud's and Angostura bitters
- ½ teaspoon of Bénédictine liqueur

METHOD: Shake all ingredients in your cocktail shaker with ice, strain, and serve in a Nick and Nora glass neat or in a rocks glass on the rocks. Garnish with a cherry.

Peychaud's bitters are made in Louisiana.

Laissez les bons temps rouler!
LET THE GOOD TIMES ROLL!
(NOTE: THIS IS STRICTLY AN EXPRESSION IN LOUISIANA, NOT FRANCE.)

THE SAZERAC BAR

130 Roosevelt Way, The Roosevelt,
New Orleans, LA 70112
Phone: (504) 648-1200
Price: **
Atmosphere: Uptown chic
http://therooseveltneworleans.com/
dining/the-sazerac-bar.html

Located in the Roosevelt hotel, this is *the* spot where the Sazerac was invented back in the 1850s. The potent combination of Herbsaint (a New World version of absinthe), Rye from America and Peychaud's bitters from New Orleans emerges as a melting pot of cultures in a glass. The bar remains stylish, uptown, and the picture-perfect place to try your first Sazerac.

BOULIGNY TAVERN

3641 Magazine St., New Orleans, LA
70115
Phone: (504) 891-1810
Price: **
Atmosphere: Mod lounge
http://boulignytavern.com/

Hipster and mid-century modern fanatics flock to this cocktail lounge on Magazine Street at all hours of the night. Try a White Melrose made with Basque cider while you tuck into their Gouda beignets, duck confit Brussels sprouts, or foie gras brioche. This is sipping and snacking in style!

FRENCH 75

813 Bienville St., New Orleans, LA
70112
Phone: (504) 523-5433
Price: **
Atmosphere: Classic through and through
https://www.arnaudsrestaurant.com/

Located in Arnaud's, one of Nola's oldest restaurants, French 75 was named one of the best bars in America by *Esquire* magazine. Picture cozy club chairs, overhead fans, servers in white coats, and dark polished wood. This is your Grandpa's bar that serves a mean French 75. A classic cocktail in a classic cocktail bar that has never gone out of style.

Jean Lafitte's Old Absinthe House 1807

240 Bourbon St., New Orleans, LA 70112

Phone: (504) 523-3181

Price: *

Atmosphere: Heavy day drinking acceptable

http://www.ruebourbon.com/oldabsinthehouse/

Oscar Wilde drank at this more-than-200-year-old watering hole in the French quarter of the most French city in America. Try the signature Absinthe House frappé in this casual pub adorned with football helmets. This is a place where locals and tourists happily meet to knock back a few. Drinking begins at 9 a.m.!

Napoleon House

500 Chartres St., New Orleans, LA 70130

Phone: (504) 524-9752

Price: *

Atmosphere: French Louisiana

http://www.napoleonhouse.com/

Created for Napoleon back in 1821 as a refuge from his troubles in France. Napoleon never ended up here but you'll feel his spirit in this dark, funky, almost decrepit bar and café. The place oozes that casual Louisianan charm, and the combo of a muffuletta sandwich (a Nola classic) and a ginger mint Pimm's Cup cocktail makes for a refreshingly delicious afternoon.

NEW YORK

There are more than 50,000 Frenchmen and women living in New York City, and most others that aren't French are huge Paris fans. So it's not surprising that in Manhattan and Brooklyn, you'll find a plethora of French-owned or -inspired places: stores, restaurants, bistros, crêperies, boulangeries, and yes, French cocktail bars.

DJ Max August of New York created this scrumptious number for my book. What a sweetie. Yes, I'm prejudiced; he's my son, but he was trained as a bartender.

- 2 oz. Grey Goose vodka
- 1 oz. St. Germain (or any elderflower liqueur)
- Juice combo made from; ½ fresh grapefruit, ½ lime and ½ lemon
- Grottissimo cherry

METHOD: Shake the above ingredients in a cocktail shaker with ice.

Strain and serve in a high-ball glass with ice, and top off with Lorina all-natural sparkling French lemonade.

SERVING SUGGESTION: Garnish with a Grottissimo cherry and a barspoon of the brandy that they come in to make it pink!

Lorina all-natural sparkling French lemonade is available at fine gourmet grocers.

This cocktail comes courtesy of Phil Ward, bartender at Death & Co., New York City.

- ◆ 2 oz. Beefeater London dry gin
- ◆ 1 oz. Dolin dry vermouth
- ◆ ½ oz. triple sec or Cointreau
- ◆ 3 dashes absinthe (Vieux Pontarlier brand is preferred)
- ◆ 1 lemon twist

METHOD: Stir all the ingredients over ice, then strain into a coupe glass.

SERVING SUGGESTION: Garnish with a lemon twist.

DAVID KAPLAN, FOUNDER OF DEATH & CO.

• • •

"OUR NAME, DEATH & CO., IS DERIVED FROM A PLAQUE FROM THE PROHIBITION ERA THAT ILLUSTRATED THAT THE SLIDE DOWNHILL STARTS AT HANGING OUT AT THE SODA FOUNTAINS AND HOTEL BARS WHICH LEADS TO COCKTAILS, DRUGS, AND DEATH."

Jessica Gonzalez from Death & Co. authored this little number.

- 2 ounces high-quality cognac (Hine brand is preferred)
- ¾ ounce Cocchi Americano
- ¾ ounce red vermouth (Dolin is preferred but any sweet vermouth may be substituted)
- 1 dash grapefruit bitters by Bittermans

METHOD: Stir all the ingredients over ice, then strain into a coupe glass. No garnish needed.

— BARON OF BROOKLYN —

Maison Premiere, a French bar in Williamsburg, is probably the most famous and difficult-to-get-into joint in this hipster enclave just across the water from Manhattan. It's only fitting, then, that they create a title such as this.

- 1 dash mole
- 1 dash Angostura bitters
- ½ oz. Suze
- ½ oz. Crème du Banane

- 1½ oz. Tawny Port
- 1½ oz. Avua cachaça (or any other premium cachaça)

METHOD: Mix everything in a cocktail class with ice, stir, strain, and serve in a brandy snifter with one large ice cube.

SERVING SUGGESTION: Garnish with a long lemon horse-neck twist.

Twists—there are several kinds. The one most of us know is the basic twist: use a pairing knife or a vegetable scraper and take some of the peel off a piece of citrus that is fairly wide and about 2 inches long max. You can then cut it down to be thinner if you wish. For a horse-neck, peel around the lemon (or other citrus) to create a spiral; these are about three times as long as a normal twist and are used when you want to start the twist down deep in the glass and or let it hang in and then over as opposed to floating on top.

MAISON PREMIERE

298 Bedford Ave., Brooklyn, NY 11211
Phone: (347) 335-0446
Price: **
Atmosphere: Where the cool "kids"
hang
http://maisonpremiere.com/

This horseshoe-shaped bar and tiny restaurant takes its inspira-tion from Chez Janou in the Marais. The classic working ab-sinthe fountain, thirty kinds of oysters, and the huge selection of absinthe on offer makes this gor-geous yet intimate bar a home-run for any of the cool kids who can squeeze their way in.

> TRICKS TO GETTING INTO MAISON PREMIERE: Open 7 days, 365 from 4 p.m. to 4 a.m. People line up at 3:30 p.m. to enjoy their $1 oyster happy hours. Don't do the same. Wait until the rush is over and head in at 5 or 5:30 p.m. on a Monday or Tuesday night, but be prepared to put your cell number down on the iPad and wait to land a stool in this always-packed hot-spot.

— MAISON ABSINTHE COLADA —

Ⓒ

A take on the classic piña colada with an absinthe twist via Maxwell Britten of Maison Premiere, Williamsburg, Brooklyn, New York.

- 1 oz. absinthe
- ½ oz. Rhum JM
  (a type of rhum agricole)
- 1 teaspoon Crème de Menthe
- 1 oz. pineapple juice
- ½ oz. lemon juice
- 1 oz. coconut syrup

METHOD: Combine ingredients and serve in a hurricane glass.

SERVING SUGGESTION: Maison Premiere serves this with a sprig of mint and a red-and-white paper straw. And for the absinthe, they use Mansinthe, the singer Marilyn Manson's own brand of absinthe made in Switzerland.

> Rhum agricole is made with fresh sugarcane juice. Industrial rum, which most of us buy, is made from molasses. For rum aficionados, rhum agricole, which has a stronger taste and flavor, is preferred and is considered an artisanal ingredient.

CHERCHE-MIDI

282 Bowery, New York, NY 10012
Phone: (212) 226-3055
Price: **
Atmosphere: Perfect if you're dreaming of Paris
http://www.cherchemidiny.com/

Sip a Wise Norman (a Calvados creation with sage) and munch on a crispy frogs leg and dream of Paris in Keith McNally's newest French-inspired bar/resto. After cocktails at the bar, why not stay awhile and sink into the kitchen's steak frites and a bottle of burgundy.

EXPERIMENTAL COCKTAIL CLUB

191 Chrystie St., New York, NY 10002
Price: **
Atmosphere: Vintage vogue
http://www.experimentalcocktail-clubny.com/

Romée De Goriainoff brought his team's unparalleled creativity to U.S. shores several years ago at their lower east side outpost of his famed Experimental Cocktail Club. Enjoy complex and creative concoctions created by the ECC team in the vintage-chic cocktail lounge and simply pretend you are in Paris.

THE TOP OF THE STANDARD

848 Washington St., New York, NY 10014
Phone: (212) 645-4646
Price: ***
Atmosphere: 40s and 50s glamour
http://www.standardhotels.com/highline/food-drink/the-top-of-the-standard

After reserving, head up to the Top of the Standard at the Standard Highline hotel for 1940s glamour and a kick-ass view of New York's skyline. It's a dressy adult-bar experience that you'd pull from your dreams of 1950s Paris and New York City.

La vérité est dans le vin.

IN WINE THERE IS TRUTH.

LOS ANGELES

Los Angeles has its own style to be sure, but even tanned Hollywood hipster types want to retreat to the old world of France some nights.

BAR BOUCHON

235 N Canon Drive, Beverly Hills, CA 90210
Phone: (310) 271-9910
Price: ***
Atmosphere: Parisian chic
http://www.thomaskeller.com/

Created by Thomas Keller of French laundry fame, this zinc bar simply reeks of Paris. Snack on truffle popcorn or the rilette of the day while sipping on a classic Moscow Mule served in the appropriate copper mug. The Provençal tile and the French waiters help transport you thousands of miles away from Beverly Hills and 90210.

LITTLE DOOR

8164 W 3rd St., Los Angeles, CA 90048
Phone: (323) 951-1210
Price: **
Atmosphere: French countryside
http://thelittledoor.com/

Whenever you ask an Angelino where to go to get your French on, they mention the Little Door. Try a Grandfather cocktail made with bourbon, calvados, and Italian vermouth, and sit outside after the main dining hours at either the new Santa Monica or their original location. Share a duck mousse pâté and enjoy the French country charm.

Rilettes are similar to pâtés but much easier to make. Meat or fish is cubed or shredded, salted, cooked over low heat, then cured with the animal's own fat and stored in a crock. Served at room temperature and spread over toast. Made with pork, salmon, or another meat—if you see rillettes on a menu, order one as quickly as possible. Fatty deliciousness.

Pour Vous

5574 Melrose Ave., Los Angeles, CA
90038

Phone: (323) 871-8699

Price: **

Atmosphere: Sexy

http://pourvousla.com/

This elegant Parisian cocktail lounge on Melrose in West Hollywood gives off a very sexy vibe. Whisper to your date that you'd like a *ménage à trois*, and he just might be fooled into thinking you didn't just order one of their French-inspired cocktails. The red banquets and fringed low-lit table lamps will get you in the mood.

SAN FRANCISCO

San Francisco has long been a town enamored with all things French. As of late, there has been a strong trend of French focused bars and brasseries. Heading up their drink menus are beaucoup de cocktails made with French absinthes, Cognacs, Chartreuse, and Calvados.

Trou Normand

140 New Montgomery St., San Francisco, CA 94105

Phone: (415) 975-0876

Price: **

Atmosphere: Northern French traditional

http://www.trounormandsf.com/

This bar and restaurant was named for the northern French tradition of a small sip of brandy, often Calvados, drunk between courses to settle the stomach and reawaken the palate—a lovely, if dangerous idea. The bar itself is stunning, the huge sketch of a female nude behind the bar compelling, and the nose-to-tail whole butchery concept terribly French. Order a classic Corpse Reviver and nosh on house-made headcheese and pork pâté with fennel.

Gaspar Brasserie

185 Sutter St., San Francisco, CA
94104
(415) 576-8800
Price: **
Atmosphere: 1950s chic
http://gasparbrasserie.com/

Try a quintessential French absinthe like Vieux Pontarlier in Gaspar's Absinthe frappe cocktail while sitting at the 1950s-inspired bar in San Fran's financial district. Stay longer to enjoy their briny oysters, magret de canard, and cassoulet beans. But whatever you do, don't order the Forget Paris cocktail; it may be tasty, but even in stunning San Francisco, Paris must never be forgotten.

Monseiur Benjamain

451 Gough St., San Francisco, CA
94102
(415) 402-2233
Price: **
Atmosphere: Opera stop
http://www.monsieurbenjamin.com/

Try the Ace with whiskey and calvados, rosemary, and gin served in a Nick and Nora era glass while chomping on some camembert beignets. This slick modern bar and restaurant is the perfect stop before a night at the Symphony or the Opera house, both of which are walking distance away.

Urchin Bistrot

584 Valencia St., San Francisco, CA
94110
(415) 861-1844
Price: **
Atmosphere: Farmhouse bistro
http://urchinbistrot.com/

Inspired by the Bistronomique movement in France, a husband-wife duo has opened this modern French bistro adding a fourth feather in their cap of culinary outposts. Belly up to the long wooden bar and order one of their artistically made, French-themed cocktails.

Bar Agricole

355 11th St., San Francisco, CA 94103
(415) 355-9400
Price: **
Atmosphere: Caribbean beach skyline
http://www.baragricole.com/

This is the place to enjoy Caribbean-made rhum agricole with more than twenty mostly French Caribbean rums on the menu. This modern, very San Francisco–styled restaurant and bar serves some of the best drinks in the country and with the skyline of San Francisco as your backdrop, you'll head home grinning.

La Folie

2316 Polk St. San Francisco, CA 94109
(415) 775-5577
Price: ***
Atmosphere: Russian Hill French
www.lafolie.com/

Depending on the time of day, order up a charcuterie plate, some salmon lollipops, or a basket of macarons to go with your Reverse Cosmosis made with St. Germain. White bar stools, cool mint walls, and a famous happy hour are the hallmarks of this popular French-feeling bar and resto.

FLORIDA

Villa Azul

309 23rd St., Miami Beach, FL 33139
(305) 763-8699
Price: **
Atmosphere: White hot
http://www.villaazurmiami.com/

Saddle up to the bar and order a French Kiss, a Veev en Rose, or Mon Cheri at this white wonderland frequented by the who's who of Miami. So stylish, you'll want to move in and make a night of it.

MAUDE'S LIQUOR BAR

840 W. Randolph St., Chicago, IL
60607
(312) 243-9712
Price: **
Atmosphere: Brooklyn-style hipster
http://www.maudesliquorbar.com/

A sparkling St. Germain fizz or a Lillet Rose will start you off at this dimly lit hipster enclave that feels more like Williamsburg, Brooklyn than Chicago. Downstairs serves more rustic fare while upstairs you'll find the finer more complex cocktails, either way you'll relish this seductive Chi-town hotspot.

LES ZYGOMATES

129 South St., Boston, MA 02111
(617) 542-5108
Price: **
Atmosphere: Wine bar cool
http://winebar129.com/

Yes, it's primarily a wine bar (Boston's finest) and a French bistro, but head to the bar and grab an Aviation with crème de Violette or their Champagne cocktail with house-made bitters and you'll understand the meaning of their name in French. Les Zygomates refers to the muscles in your face that allow you to smile.

"YOU CAN LEARN A LOT ABOUT A WOMAN BY GETTING SMASHED WITH HER."

Tom Waits

MINNESOTA

Coup D'Etat

2923 Girard Ave. S., Minneapolis, MN 55408

(612) 354-3575

Price: **

Atmosphere: Minnesota party

http://coupdetatmpls.com/

Emperor Napoleon hangs proudly in this huge, double-decker bar, restaurant, and party space in Minneapolis. Jesse, the head bartender, is considered the finest in the region, and the bar was named one of the best new openings in 2014, countrywide. The Ritz cocktail and grilled oysters with Pernod butter will make a homesick Francophile swoon.

PENNSYLVANIA

The Good King Tavern

614 S. 7th St., Philadelphia, PA 19147

(215) 625-3700

Price: *

Atmosphere: Casual pub

http://thegoodkingtavern.com/

Old wooden bar, rustic French feel, tavern Fare, and classic French cocktails on offer. Settle into a French 75 or a Sazerac and let your hair down. Their motto: A whole lotta soul, some hip, some hop, and a really good time.

JULEP

1919 Washington Ave., Houston, TX
77707
(713) 869-4383
Price: **
Atmosphere: Southern French
www.julephouston.com/

Considered one of the best bars to open in 2014, this gorgeously posh France-meets-the-south bar looks fresh and summery year round. They specialize in the oh-so-southern mint julep in every contortion. But owner and cocktail maven Alba Huerta also offers an Armagnac Sazerac, a Vieux Carré, and a Brandied French for those pining for Paris.

BOULEVARDIER

408 N. Bishop Ave., Dallas, TX 75208
(214) 942-1828
Price: **
Atmosphere: A loft in Texas
http://dallasboulevardier.com/

Head to this French-inspired bar and bistro that serves oysters alongside their Raised & Infused cocktail that highlights gin, thyme, Cointreau, and absinthe. The perfect way to start a night out on the town in Dallas's arts district.

WASHINGTON STATE

BASTILLE BAR

5307 Ballard Ave., Seattle, WA 98107
(206) 453-5014
Price: **
Atmosphere: Subway tile bistro
http://bastilleseattle.com/

Head to the back bar, with its huge French chandelier and chocolate colored walls for a stylish night out in Seattle. Sample the Millionaire's punch with bourbon, absinthe, and grenadine, and slurp down some local oysters.

This cocktail comes to us from the maker of Chartreuse Verte but was invented in Detroit in 1920 at the Detroit Athletic club during Prohibition. It was forgotten about until Murray Stensen, a well-known bartender at the Zig Zag bar in Seattle, found it and brought it back into the current repertoire.

- ½ oz. Chartreuse Verte
- ½ oz. Maraschino liqueur (Luxardo preferred)
- ½ oz. gin
- ½ oz. lime

METHOD: Pour all ingredients into a cocktail shaker with ice.

SERVING SUGGESTION: Shake, strain, and serve in a cold coupe glass garnishing with a lime curl.

La vie est belle.

LIFE IS BEAUTIFUL.

— RAISING THE BAR:

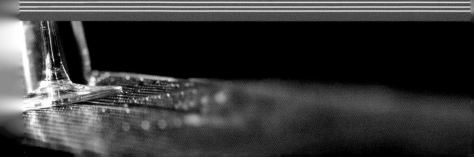

BEST OF THE BEST —

Pretend for a moment that you are watching one of those competitive cooking shows. As I was finishing up this project I was going over in my mind what drink was the tastiest, what bartender the most inventive, and what bars had the best ambiance. While it was never meant to be a competition, below I give you The All-Stars.

BEST DRINK I TASTED: The incredible L'Apicius Bloody Mary. All I can say is: Oh my God! A Bloody Mary without any citrus and made with muddled fresh cherry tomatoes, this one blew me away. See Most Creative Bartender below.

TOP 5 BARTENDERS: Valentin, L'Apicius; Joseph, Baton Rouge; Amanda, Pas de Loup; Kaled, Andy Wahloo; Alessandro, the Royal Monceau Hotel.

MOST CREATIVE BARTENDER: Valentin, l'Apicius. Not only does he make one of the best drinks I've had in Paris (see page 54 for his version of the Bloody Mary), but he'll create a bespoke cocktail just for you when you come to his bar.

MOST AMAZING FRENCH COCKTAIL HISTORIAN: Stephen Miller from À la Française.

MOST IMPRESSIVE PRESENTATION OF A DRINK: L'Education Sentimentale at Shake N' Smash.

The drink, a mixture of ingredients from Normandy, including Calvados and alcoholic cider, was served in a snifter placed on its side on a bowl of crushed ice with a fan of caramelized, thin apple slices sticking out of the ice as well as a cinnamon stick. This entire get-up was placed on a page of the book by Flaubert, the drink's namesake, which had been slightly burned on the edges. Only in France would you see such an intellectual presentation for what was a very tasty drink highlighting all that Normandy has to offer.

MOST CREATIVE SOMMELIER: Michael Cohen from Le Perchoir, the hipster rooftop bar and resto in the 11th.

MOST *GENTILLE* (NICE) BAR OWNERS: Nico and Melissa from Bespoke on rue Oberkampf. And their dog Bruce is a real cutie, too!

- Acknowledgments -

First I'd like to thank my editor, Alex Lewis of Cider Mill Press, who at a young age is the publishing director at an independent publishing firm in Maine. She picked me out of a sea of wonderful writers on the subject, thanks to the huge audience of Girls' Guide to Paris readers. So, in turn, I must thank our 1+ million readers who put our online Paris e-guide on the map. Alex was with me throughout giving creative suggestions and letting me immerse myself in the exciting new world of Parisian cocktails. I must also thank my intern and research assistant Ariana Mozafari who was critical to my being able to finish this book. It wouldn't have been nearly as fun without her by my side and at the bar.

Most of all I must thank my family: my husband, who is the finest male supporter of a female that has ever graced the earth, and my two twenty-something kids, who keep me current and support me in everything I do. Getting paid to drink and write about cocktails in Paris was truly a dream come true.

- INDEX -

CELEBRATIONS

Midnight in Paris Party, 23
Provençal Party, 64
Sparkling Fête, 80–81
Jazz Era Celebration, 103
Make Your Own Cocktail Friday,
    146–147
Joyeuse Noel Fête, 162
An Artisanal Drinks Tasting Party,
    176–177
Mardi Gras Fête, 236–237

RECIPES

100% Winter Vitamin, 49
14 Julliet, 126
1789, 125
23 Jump Street, 97
Alchimia Cocktail, 37
Amour à la Française, 20
Audemus Century, 214
Aviation, 94
B&B, 45
Baron of Brooklyn, 247
Bastille Celebration, The, 82
Bastille Sour, The, 115

Bisous du Soleil, 68
Black Point à la Française, 197
Bloody Secret, 187
Bloody Umami, 139
Bobo Parisien, 196
Bramble & Queen, 113
Brenne Hot Toddy, 166
Canapés, 177
Capri C'est Fini, 184
Cerise Sour, 145
Chamber G&T, The, 98
Chartreuse Mule, 161
Choco Peat, 123
Coffee Old Fashioned, 224
Corpse Reviver, No. 2, 84
Cranberry Sparkler, 165
De la Bretagne, 190
Education Sentimental, 168
Equisse No. 1, 218
Experiénce 1, 192
Façon Maria, 226
Faluka, 188
Forum Cocktail, 114
French 75 Squared, 95
French 75, 30

French Manhattan, The, 116
French Martini de Nancy, 150
French Negroni, 131
French Old Fashioned, The, 104
French Open Pimm's Cup, 128
Fuego de Colima, 217
Highland Cream, 130
Iced Tea Peyi, 62
Iggy, 205
Incredible Apicius Bloody Mary, The, 54
Jennifer's Slipper, 152
Joy Division, 245
L'Orange Passion, 149
La Conquistador, 221
Lady B, 118
Lafayette, The, 109
Last Call, The, 153
Last Word, The, 259
Le Bon Chic Bon Genre (BCBG), 117
Le Grand's Original Dry Martini, 129
Le Metro, 27
Le Pulpeux, 222
Le Woody Wood, 227
Léa D'Asco, 110
Libertine, 212
Macaroni Cocktail. 67
Maison Absinthe Colada, 249
Mardi Gras Wine Cocktails, 237
Mazarinette, 209
Mistinguette, 100
Moonflower, 207
Night Bird, 213

Oh My Dog, 48
Old Cuban, 193
Original Bloody Mary Recipe, The, 122
Oysters on the Half Shell, 81
Park Hyatt Purple Mojito, 41
Peruvian Shrub, 43
Picasso Martini, 136
Pink Panther, 243
Piste Verte, 160
Pomegranate Margarita, 169
PPR, 151
Raphael, 57
Red House Old Fashioned, 211
Ritz Sidecar, 33
Romeo à Rio, 199
Rose Cosmo, 28
Rose de Varsovie, 71
Rose Salty Dog, 31
Rosebud, 184
Sade's Taboo, 246
Sazerac, 238
Serendipiti, 83
Singapore Sling, 107
Smoky Spicy Margarita, The, 200
Soirée, The, 144
Suze and Soda, 24
Sweet Pea, 108
Tijuana Swizzle, 44
Umami Martini, 137
Verbena Cocktail, 38
Verdant Martini, 135
Vieux Carré, 239
Vin Chaud, 164
Whiskey Sour Cerise, 234

Yazu Corn, 175
Year of the Frenchman, The, 120
Zeitouni, 179

BARS
À la Française, 180
Amuse Bouche, 228
Andy Wahloo, 178
Bar 228 at the Meurice, 35
Bar Agricole, 255
Bar Bouchon, 252
Bastille Bar, 258
Baton Rouge, 219
Bespoke, 180
Best of the Best, 262-263
Boulevardier, 258
Bouligny Tavern, 240
Café Moderne, 183
Canadian bars
    Montreal, 228
    Toronto, 229
    Vancouver, 229
Candelaria, 183
Castor Club, 184
Chamber, The, 225
Cherche-Midi, 251
Chez Nous, 87
Chez Prune, 50
Ciel de Paris, 50
Clown Bar, 87
Companie sur Vin Naturels, 89
Comptoir Generale, 219
Copper Bay, 184
Coup d'etat, 257
Craft bars, 178, 180, 183, 186, 191,

194, 198, 200, 203, 204, 206,
    208, 210, 216
Death & Co., 244–45
Death by Burrito, 223
Dive Bars, 154–155
Experimental Cocktail Club (ECC),
    London, 228
Experimental Cocktail Club (ECC),
    New York, 251
Experimental Cocktail Club (ECC),
    Paris, 191
French 75, 140
Gaspar Brassiere, 254
Georges V, 34
Glass, 194
Good King Tavern, The, 258
Gossima Ping Pong Bar, 220
Harry's New York Bar, 121
Hemingway Bar at the Ritz Bar, 127
Historic Bars, 120, 127
Hotel Bars, 34–36, 40, 46
Hôtel Particulier Bar, 69
Jean LaFitte's Old Absinthe House
    1807, 141
Jefrey's, 194
Julep, 258
Kir St. Louis, 76
L'Apicius, 51
L'Ebiniste du Vin, 89
L'Éclair, 53
L'Éntrée des Artistes, 203
La Belle Hortense, 50
La Conserverie, 198
La Folie en Tête, 155
La Folie, 255

La Recyclerie, 51
La Société (LS), 229
Lapérouse, 51
Le Baron Rouge, 88
Le Calbar, 198
Le Charlie, 154
Le Grand Hotel, 127
Le Lab, 228
Le Mary Celeste, 201
Le Mini Palais, 69
Le Perchoir, 69
Le Quatre, 46
Le Royal Monceau, 36
Le Syndicat, 203
Les Idiots, 155
Les Pères Populaires, 155
Les Zygomates, 256
Little Door, 252
Little Red Door, 204
London, 228
Lulu White, 206
Mabel, 204
Madame Rouge, 78
Maison Premiere, 247
Maria Loca, 225
Maude's Liquor Bar, 256
Monsieur Benjamin, 254
Napoleon House, 241
Park Hyatt Vendome, 40
Pas de Loup, 208
Peninsula Hotel, 35
Pour Vous, 253
Prescription Cocktail Club, 208
Raphael Terrace, 56
Red House, 210

Rosebud, 131
Rosé-Pamp, 77
Sazerac Bar, The, 240
Shake N' Smash, 216
Shangri-La, 34
Sherry Cherie, 79
Superb Ambiance, 50–53, 56
Tableau Bar & Bistro, 229
Top of the Standard, The, 251
Trou Normand, 253
Unique bars, 219, 220, 223, 225,
    228, 229
Urchin Bistrot, 254
U.S. Bars
    Boston, 256
    Chicago, 256
    Dallas, 258
    Houston, 258
    Los Angeles, 252–253
    Miami Beach, 255
    Minneapolis, 257
    New Orleans, 240, 241
    New York, 242–251
    Philadelphia, 257
    San Francisco, 253–255
    Seattle, 258
Views Worth Drinking To, 69
Villa Azul, 255
Wall St. Bar, 223
Wine bars, 87–89

Doni Belau first saw Paris at the tender age of eighteen and fell in love. She has been regularly visiting or living in her favorite city ever since. In 2009, Ms. Belau founded the website www.GirlsGuidetoParis.com, an insider's guide to the city of light. The site includes her hand-picked favorite restaurants, bars, hotels, apartments, and activities to experience Paris like a native. It also features blogs written by Ms. Belau and many other contributors, D.I.Y. walking tours, and the popular GO-Card for Paris-bound travelers. After six years, the site has grown to 1.5 million readers per year and is one of the foremost Anglophone guides for travelers to France. In 2014, Doni authored the online guidebook EAT in Paris. She divides her time between New York City, Paris, and the Bordeaux region, where she shares a home with her husband and two grown children.

- ABOUT CIDER MILL PRESS BOOK PUBLISHERS -

Good ideas ripen with time. From seed to harvest, Cider Mill Press brings fine reading, information, and entertainment together between the covers of its creatively crafted books. Our Cider Mill bears fruit twice a year, publishing a new crop of titles each spring and fall.

VISIT US ON THE WEB AT
www.cidermillpress.com

OR WRITE TO US AT
12 Spring Street
PO Box 454
Kennebunkport, Maine 04046

Chapelle Expiatoire

Mag. du Printemps

Temple

R. Rich.

Temple Prot.

Musée Grévin

ere de rieur

Marché de la Madeleine

B. Montm.

Opéra

Place de l'Opéra

B. des Italiens

Opéra Comique

Th. des Variétés

Rue de Surène

Grand Hôtel

Lavoisier

Temple Anglican

Madeleine

B. des Capucines

Pl. et Pal. de la Bourse

R. de la Madne

bassade leterre

Marché

R. de la Mad

R. de la Paix

Crédit Foncier

Banque de France (Annexe)

Bibliothèque Nationale

Min. de la Justice

Place Colonne Vendôme

R. des

N.D. des Victoires

Concert Ambass

Place

Min. de la Marine

St H.

Cirque Now

Marché St. Hon.

Pl. des Victoires

Ludw. XIV

Obélisque de la

Jardin de

St Roch

R. Molière

Banque de France

Hô des P.

Téléph.

Concorde

Orangerie

Tuileries

J. d'Arc

Théâtre Français

Palais Royal

Bourse du Commerce

Quai

orps islatif

Ambassade d'Allemagne

Arc de Triomphe du Carrousel

Place du Carrousel

Magasin du Louvre

Coligny

Pal.

Légion d'Honneur

Min. d. Finan.

Palais du Louvre

Minist. des Colonies

St Germ.

Minist. de la Guerre

Gare du Quai d'Orsay (d'Orléans)

St Germ. l'Auxerrois

St Clotilde

Quai

Quai du Louvre

Rue de Lille

Henri IV

Minist. des Trav. Publ.

École des Beaux Arts

Palais de l'Institut

Hôtel des Monnaies

Pal. de Jus

St Thomas

Temple protest.

Dépôt de l'Artille

École des Ponts et Chaussées

Ambassade de Russie

Chappe

Hôpital de la Charité

Ambassade d'Autriche-Hongrie

St Germain d'Prés

Pl. St Mic

Missions Étrangères

Babylone

Marché St Germain

Danton

École de Médecine

Soeurs St Vinc. de Paul

Square Mag. du Bon Marché

Prison Milit.

Pl. St Sulpice

St Sulpice

École Pratique

Musée

Hôpital

Caserne